HORRIBLE SCIENCE

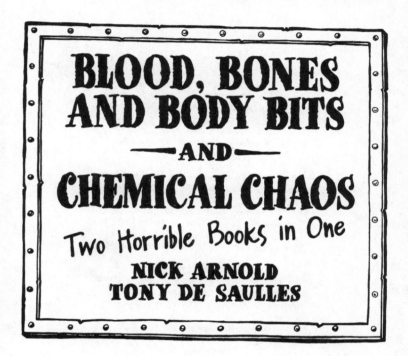

BLOOD, BONES AND BODY BITS

—AND—

CHEMICAL CHAOS

Two Horrible Books in One

NICK ARNOLD
TONY DE SAULLES

■SCHOLASTIC

Scholastic Children's Books,
Commonwealth House, 1-19 New Oxford Street,
London WC1A 1NU, UK

A division of Scholastic Ltd
London ~ New York ~ Toronto ~ Sydney ~ Auckland
Mexico City ~ New Delhi ~ Hong Kong

Published in this edition by Scholastic Ltd, 1998
Cover illustration copyright © Tony De Saulles, 1998

Blood, Bones and Body Bits
First published in the UK by Scholastic Ltd, 1996
Text copyright © Nick Arnold, 1996
Illustrations copyright © Tony De Saulles, 1996

Chemical Chaos
First published in the UK by Scholastic Ltd, 1997
Text copyright © Nick Arnold, 1997
Illustrations copyright © Tony De Saulles, 1997

ISBN 0 590 54365 2

Printed by WSOY, Finland

10 9 8 7 6 5 4 3 2 1

The right of Nick Arnold and Tony De Saulles to be identified as the author and
illustrator of this work respectively has been asserted by them in accordance
with the Copyright, Designs and Patents Act, 1988.

Contents

Blood, Bones and Body Bits

Chemical Chaos

BLOOD, BONES AND BODY BITS

Nick Arnold has been writing stories and books since he was a youngster, but never dreamt he'd find fame writing about Horrible Science. His research involved inspecting sick, encountering deadly diseases and being blown up and he enjoyed every minute of it.

When he's not delving into Horrible Science, Nick spends his spare time teaching adults in a college. His hobbies include eating pizza, riding his bike and thinking up corny jokes (though not all at the same time).

Tony De Saulles picked up his crayons when he was still in nappies and has been doodling ever since. He takes Horrible Science very seriously and even agreed to investigate what happens in an operating theatre and how explosives work. Fortunately, he has made a full recovery.

When he's not out with his sketchpad, Tony likes to write poetry and play squash, though he hasn't written any poetry about squash yet.

HORRIBLE SCIENCE

Science with the squishy bits left in!

Also available:

Ugly Bugs
The insect world goes under the magnifying glass.
Observe some foul families of bugs, discover the
secrets of strange scientists and test the theories of
insect disguise. It's swarming with info!

Nasty Nature
Have a whale of a time finding out about the animal
world! Grapple with some very ferocious creatures,
meet some nosey naturalists and learn how to get on
with a gorilla. You'll be howling for more!

Sounds Dreadful
Lift the lid on noise and find out how sound waves
make your ear drums tremble, how a microphone turns
your voice into electrical pulses ... and why you might
get a nose bleed listening to church bells. It's a real
scream!

Disgusting Digestion
Get the inside details on your insides! Find out how
much pee your bladder can hold without popping, what
disease makes your eyeballs bleed and why astronauts
can't eat beans before a space flight.

Fatal Forces

Can you resist the urge to discover why your *ears* stop you falling off your bike? You'll also find out what keeps the moon in the sky, how quickly your fingernails grow ... and what happens when an apple smacks a scientist on the bonce!

Look out for:

Vicious Veg

Get stuck into a feast of info. and discover which plants eat dead insects for breakfast, why stinging nettles grow on old skeletons and which fungi can make your toes drop off. It's bloomin' amazing!

Bulging Brains

Get your head round some amazing brain facts. Find out what your brain smells like, how some people drill holes into their skulls and why your brain never, ever goes to sleep even when *you* do.

Science has never been so horrible!

INTRODUCTION

Science is sickening! Extra science homework is really rotten – but one of the most horribly sickening science subjects is the science of the body. I mean, doesn't the thought of all that blood and all those guts and bones turn your legs into jelly?

Doctors and teachers use a sickening selection of tongue-twisting names for bits you didn't even know you had. By the way – did you know that medical students have to learn 10,000 new words? And you thought English lessons were tough!

But science doesn't just belong to the experts – it belongs to everybody, because everybody's got a body – and you've got every right to know what's going on in yours. Why it gurgles and creaks and squelches and other tantalising topics.

And that's what this book is about. The things YOU really want to know about YOUR body. The horrible bits. The horribly interesting bits. Here's your chance to find out what billions of germs are doing lurking in your guts. What happens when you cut a brain in half, and why doctors once covered their patients in slimy leeches. So if you find science a closed book – here's a chance to change your mind.

And once you've boned up on bones and got the inside story on your insides – who knows? You might even find the body horribly amazing. Then you could teach your doctor a thing or two. Or even blind your teachers with some really sickening scientific facts. (That doesn't mean doing nasty things to their eyeballs!) One thing is certain. Science will never be the same again!

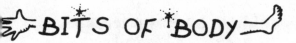

BITS OF BODY

A disgusting discovery

It was past midnight and the rain was splattering against the window-pane of the lonely attic room. By the dim light of a candle Baron Frankenstein gazed in horror at the creature that he had just put together from bits of chopped-up dead bodies. The monster was unbelievably, hideously ugly. Suddenly a shudder seemed to run through the creature's body and it stirred like a heavy sleeper about to wake. . .

DON'T PANIC! It's only a story. Frankenstein was written by Mary Shelley nearly 200 years ago and no one has succeeded in making an entire human being out of bits of body . . . yet. But just supposing you wanted to have a go, here's a bit of advice. . .

STEP ONE – GET HOLD OF A HUMAN BODY. I STOLE MOST OF MY BODY BITS . . .

If this sounds too gruesome to be true, remember that in the Baron's time there was a serious shortage of bodies to cut up. In many countries this grisly practice was against the law. This was a problem because scientists could only probe the secrets of the human body by the dissection – cutting up – of dead bodies. In desperation, some scientists turned to crime.

The Baron's guide to body-snatching

Body-snatchers were people who went about stealing bodies. The body-snatchers knew that doctors would pay handsomely for a nice fresh corpse to cut up. Here's how to get hold of one yourself (and make some extra pocket money).

Method 1 – execute a robbery. This was the method used by Andreas Versalius, a famous 16th-century scientist, when he was living in the old town of Louvain in Belgium.

1 Wait until dark.

2 Go to a nearby place of execution and remove the corpses of any criminals you find.

3 Cut up the body and hide bits of it under your cloak. That way you can smuggle it all past the guards on the city gates without anyone asking awkward questions.

4 You can hide the bits of body in your bedroom and put them together later.

If you can't find any bodies lying around things get a tiny bit more difficult.

Method 2 – rob a grave. This method was used in both Britain and America in the 19th century.

1 Wait until dark. You will need a wooden spade for silent digging, a lantern, a canvas sheet, some ropes with hooks attached, a crowbar and a sack.

2 Go to a graveyard. Make sure you keep an eye out for angry relatives, vicars, etc. who might just try to stop you digging up the bodies.

3 Dig up the grave. Spread the dug earth on the sheet ready for you to shovel it all back again afterwards. This avoids making a mess that might give you away.

4 Lift the coffin with the hooks, then lever open the coffin using the crowbar. Sssh! Keep it quiet!

5 Put the body in the sack. Fill in the hole and run for it. You should be able to do all this in an hour. Oh, and don't forget the sheet!

Body jigsaws

Let's imagine that by hook or by crook you managed to get hold of some bits of body. Now you can start putting them all together to make your very own Frankenstein's monster! Unlike a normal jigsaw, you have to start with the middle bits, not the edge (the skin!). Make sure you put all the pieces in the right places and don't forget any vital parts or it won't work. If you make a mistake you will have to cut the body open and take a few bits out in order to fit the missing bit in its proper place. Here's a list of body bits to help you know what's what in your body.

Stretchy skin

A huge waterproof, germ-proof outer covering. It's better than any other kind of clothing because it actually repairs itself when it gets damaged. It also has its own heating and cooling systems. Skin wraps round the rest of the body bits to keep them in position.

Fabulous fat

Fit a layer of fat snugly underneath the skin. Slabs of fat also slop and wobble around the tummy and hips area. Fat keeps out the cold. It acts as a convenient place for storing spare sugar from all those sweets your monster eats. Your monster will use up some of the sugar when it goes for its morning jog.

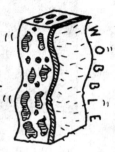

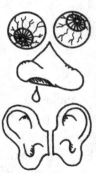

Eyeballs, ears and snotty nose

Very important for seeing, hearing and sniffing (in that order). In fact the really important bits of these body parts are the bits you can't see. These form the high-tech gadgetry that converts the information picked up from the senses into signals for the brain to de-code. So make sure those nerves are all properly wired up.

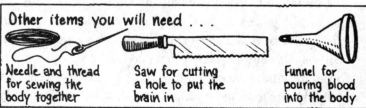

Other items you will need . . .

Needle and thread for sewing the body together

Saw for cutting a hole to put the brain in

Funnel for pouring blood into the body

Delicate nerves

These are the monster's signalling system. They tell the brain what's going on and transmit orders from the brain to get those lazy muscles moving. Nerves extend into every part of the body – from the top of the head to the tips of the toes. But the main nerves all join up in the spinal cord inside the backbone.

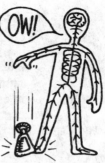

Brilliant brain

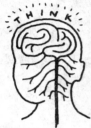

This bit acts as the boss of the monster's body. Gently plop it inside the top part of the skull, nicely protected from the outside world. It contains all your monster's memories and personality so don't bash it around too much.

Sturdy skeleton

There are 206 bones – give or take a few extra ones that some people have. Bones are very important to keep the body upright and stop it collapsing like a deflated balloon. Make sure you get the bones in the right order. This is very tricky, especially when you get to the 26 bones that make up a single foot.

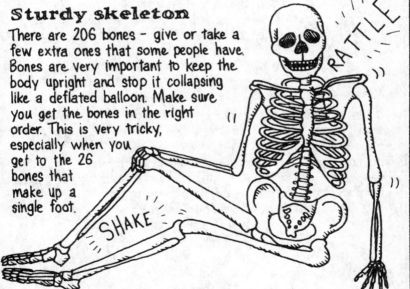

BULGE

AWFUL
UNDERPANTS

Mighty muscles

Everyone's got muscles even if they're not big bulgy ones. There are hundreds of muscles and they need to be put in their rightful places or they won't work properly. In each hand there are twenty muscles – and your monster will use 200 muscles every time it takes a step.

Tough teeth

These are the hardest parts of the body – guaranteed to tackle those rubbery school dinners. Make sure you put the teeth in their correct positions and teach your monster how to brush them regularly.

Disgusting stomach

It's a squelchy muscular bag filled with bits of half-digested food and stomach juices. Lovely! But it's vital for mashing up food so your monster can digest its dinner more easily.

GLUG GLUG WOBBLE

Lovely liver

It's a brownish/purplish/reddish blob about 15cm thick. Lovely. This is your monster's built-in chemical factory and it performs over 500 different jobs. It's called the liver because no-one can 'liver' long without it, ha ha. Pop the liver in its place over the guts under the dome of the diaphragm (that's your breathing muscle).

WIBBLE WOBBLE

Clever kidneys

These filter the blood and take out the waste products from your monster's body. It's got two kidneys and the one on the left-hand side of the body is always higher up than the right one.

Beautiful blood

It's the body's transport system, and it carries oxygen gas breathed in through the lungs and little bits of food to nourish the body. And that's just for starters. There are also white cells that fight germs and platelets that help the body heal itself. Yes – blood's got the lot. Your monster will need about 5 –5½ litres (9–10 pints) of the gloopy red stuff.

Hardworking heart

This lump of muscle is vital for pumping the blood around the body. Make sure you put the heart in its correct place – nearer the right side of the chest. Also make sure you get it the correct way round – the left-hand side of the heart pumps the blood round the body, but the right side only pumps it round the lungs.

PUMP

Foamy lungs

These are like a big spongy pair of bellows in the chest that can hold up to six litres of air. Your monster needs to breathe in order to get the oxygen from the air to keep its body cells alive.

BREATHE

15

Weird bits 'n' pieces

Some bits of the body are well known. We've all heard about the brain and we've all heard from the stomach when it starts rumbling. But what about the not-so-well-known bits? Which of these bits are just too weird to be true? (You get double the score if you can work out where any of them fit in!)

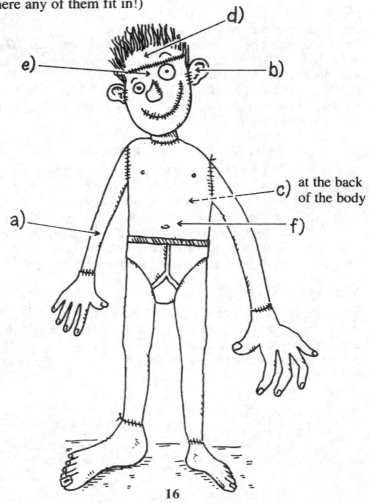

d)

e)

b)

a)

c) at the back of the body

f)

16

1 The oval window
2 The funny bone
3 The innominate canal of Arnold
4 The wish bone
5 The boomerang bone
6 Fabricus's ship
7 The bicycle tendon
8 Lane's kinks
9 Morris's kidney box
10 The fossa of Blumenbach

Is everything working?

Whilst you are assembling your Frankenstein's monster, it's always a good idea to occasionally check that the bits of body are in good shape. You can do this by peering down a microscope and making sure the cells are still alive. . .

Secret cells

Your body is made up of about 100 billion living cells. You can tell when they are alive because there are all sorts of chemical changes going on inside them. Every cell is like a tiny ball of jelly full of chemicals and it's far too small to see without a microscope. In fact, you can squeeze thousands of them into the full stop at the end of this sentence.

Inside the cell is a secret world. There are tiny objects called mitochondria (mito-con-dre-a) that produce energy, and there are pathways and little storage areas. And each cell has a nucleus that stores the information to make new cells. Sometimes the cell reproduces by pulling itself into two pieces.

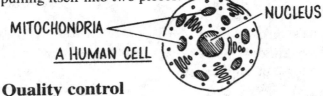

MITOCHONDRIA

NUCLEUS

A HUMAN CELL

Quality control
Once your Frankenstein's monster is assembled you'll need a collection of amazing but slightly gruesome tools to check whether everything is in working order inside.

X-rays
Some of the devices below use X-rays. These are a special kind of light ray that you can't actually see. X-rays can pass through the body's skin, muscles and fat but not solid bone. This is why an X-ray picture can check out whether the bones are in good shape.

18

CAT – computerised axial tomography scanner. This amazing machine scans a slice of your monster's brain using X-rays and shows the result on a computer screen. Angiogram (An-gy-o-gram) An X-ray picture of your monster's blood vessels after they have been injected with chemicals.

Then there are a whole collection of tubes to stick into various parts of its anatomy so you can take a look at it. These include. . .

Gastroscope (gas-tro-scope) A long, bendy tube with a light on the end. Ideal for poking down its throat to see into its stomach and guts.

Ophthalmoscope (op-thal-mo-scope) A bright light and viewer to see what the inside of its eyeball looks like.

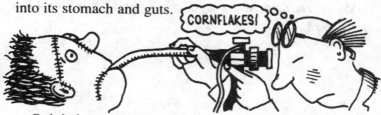

Arthroscope (ar-throw-scope) A tube a bit like a telescope for peering inside your creature's joints.

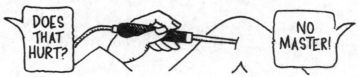

Otoscope (ot-o-scope) A light a bit like a torch for shining in your monster's ear-holes.

All these bits of equipment are useful because without them it's horribly hard to see what's going on inside the body. There's usually a layer of sweaty skin in the way. Let's take a longer look at it. . .

SWEATY SKIN

Poke around in the darker corners of your house and you may find a lovely collection of fingernails, hair and bits of skin. Bits of skin? Well – you know those pretty bits of dust that dance in the sunlight on a summer's morning? Most of them are bits of flaked-off skin – just some of the ten billion bits of skin you lose every day!

Skin fact file

Name of body part: Skin

Where found: All over the outside of the body

Useful things it does: It helps to keep you at the right temperature and keep out germs.

Grisly details: It suffers from a disgusting array of skin diseases such as boils, carbuncles, etc.

Amazing features: If you removed an adult's skin it would cover about 2 square metres (2.4 square yards). A child's skin covers about 1.5 square metres. Skin is the heaviest part of your body and weighs a whopping 2.5-4.5kg (5-10lbs), depending on your size.

Disgusting skin diseases

Doctors like nothing better than reading at mealtimes. And their favourite reading matter? Colourful medical magazines with pictures of skin diseases. Gulp! Here's your chance to check whether you could be a doctor. Try matching the picture to the disease:

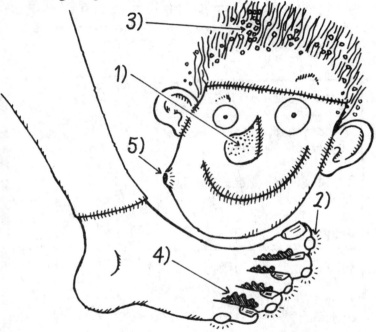

a) A fungus that grows between the toes and makes the skin peel.

b) A gland-opening that's been blocked with sweat or grease – it swells until it bursts, spraying pus everywhere.

c) Painful, itchy blotches on your toes caused by the blood supply cutting off in cold weather.

d) A build up of dead skin cells stuck together with grease.

e) Greasy dead skin cells that turn black when they come in contact with the air.

Nasty nose jobs

If your skin disease gets really revolting you could have plastic surgery to replace some of it.

Bet you never knew!
Modern plastic surgeons make changes to the surface of the body – adding or taking away skin in order to change what someone looks like. If you've got enough money, you can change almost any part of your body. But plastic surgery actually began in India about 2,000 years ago! Criminals were punished by having their noses cut off but one day someone found out that you could stitch some skin from the forehead or cheek over the wound so it didn't look so bad. In Sicily, Italy, they took the idea one stage further. A sinister surgeon named Branca cut off a slave's nose and sewed it onto one of his patients who had lost his own nose in a battle! Modern plastic surgeons make changes to the surface of the body – adding or taking away skin in order to change someone's appearance. These operations are called "skin grafts".

23

But if skin can be amazingly horrible on the outside – on the inside it's also horribly AMAZING.

Getting under your skin

If you removed an adult's skin (a very messy job) it would cover about two square metres (2.4 square yards). A child's skin covers about 1.5 square metres (1.8 square yards). Skin is the heaviest part of your body and weighs a whopping 2.5-4.5 kg (5-10 lbs) depending on your size. That's as heavy as a bag stuffed with food from a supermarket! But the outer layer of your skin is less than 1 mm thick. Even so, it's packed with sensors for hot and cold, and blood vessels and fat and cells for producing sweat and so on. Confusing isn't it? Try imagining your skin as an incredible high-tech, high-fashion space suit. Would you dare to wear it?

The Birthday Suit

Have YOU ever wished to slip into something more comfortable? Something that's cool in hot weather and warm in cold weather. Try the new birthday suit. But guess what - you've got it on already! Yes, it's that suit you got for your birthday – that's the day you were born!

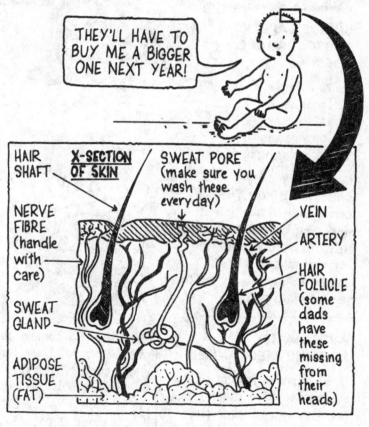

Marvel at these incredible features. Amaze your friends with THE BIRTHDAY SUIT's unique technical wizardry!

The amazing
BIRTHDAY SUIT

UNIQUE SAFETY PHOTOCHROMIC COLOURS

GET ONE FREE WITH EVERY NEWBORN BABY!

1. Your BIRTHDAY SUIT comes in a variety of colours all provided by its unique melanin pigments.

2. Ordinary clothes fade in the sunshine but your BIRTHDAY SUIT comes with a guaranteed darkening action under sunlight to protect the wearer from harmful rays. It actually creates extra melanin for this all-important purpose.

NO FADING

FRONT

CHOICE OF COLOURS

AUTOMATIC COOLING MECHANISM

3. This unique feature springs into action if the suit gets too hot. The water-cooling pipes produce sweat to cool the outside of the BIRTHDAY SUIT.

4. Every BIRTHDAY SUIT is guaranteed to contain about three million of these tiny water-cooling pipes (known as sweat glands) and each one is so tightly coiled that if you pulled it out it would be over a metre long! The total length of your pipe system is 50km (31 miles)!

26

5. The automatic cooling systems can easily lose 1.7 litres (quarter of a gallon) of sweat every hour in hot weather, so make sure it's well supplied with water.

6. The sweat under the arms and between the legs contains chemicals that germs like to eat. Yum! The germs make the stale sweat all yucky and smelly. (Please see Care and maintenance instruction 9 – for everybody's sake.)

7. Some people use deodorants to tackle the little problem above. These work by blocking the holes in the cooling systems. Fortunately they don't stop most of the sweat from escaping otherwise the BIRTHDAY SUIT would overheat.

SELF-REPAIRING MECHANISM

AUTOMATIC COOLING SYSTEM

BACK

LOW MAINTENANCE

HARMFUL RAY PROTECTION

9. All you need to do is to gently wash the outer layer in soap and water to remove any dirt and flaky bits. Don't worry if bits drop off – the BIRTHDAY SUIT will always grow some more underneath!

CARE & MAINTENANCE INSTRUCTIONS

8. Your BIRTHDAY SUIT needs very little maintenance because of its unique self-repair mechanism. If it gets torn or damaged it will simply re-grow!

Dare you find out for yourself . . . how your skin works?

For this experiment you will have to take a hot bath. It's OK – all the great scientists had to make sacrifices.

1 Note what happens as your skin heats up. What colour does it go?

a) Red

b) Blue

c) White

2 Using a watch, time how long it takes for your skin to wrinkle up. As a result of your careful scientific observation, what do you think is causing this strange effect?

a) The heat

b) Old age

c) The water

Answers 1 a) The colour is due to the blood vessels that run under the skin widening to allow more blood in. This helps release heat through the skin and cools your over-heating body! **2 c)** Your skin is covered by a layer of oily grease called sebum that keeps the water out. But after a while some of the water seeps through and makes the under layer waterlogged. This crumples up the top layer causing wrinkles. It's a bad idea to let too much water get under the skin. The cells absorb all the water they can until they explode! Lucky your hair and nails are not affected.

HORRIBLE HAIR AND NASTY NAILS

What's the point of hair and nails? Hairs always seem to end up blocking the bathroom plug hole and nails get nasty black grime stuck underneath them. But then they're also interesting in a disgusting kind of way.

Hair and nails fact file

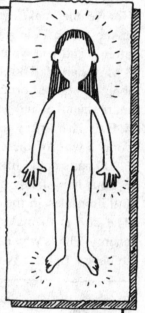

Name of body part: Hair and nails

Where found: Your body is covered by five million little hairs but your longest hairs are on your head (surprisingly!). Nails are found on your fingers and toes, but you knew that.

Useful things they do: Hair keeps you warm. Your nails stop your fingers and toes squashing up every time you touch something.

Grisly details: Hair and nails are said to continue to grow for a while on dead bodies.

Amazing features: Hair and nails are both made out of a hard substance called keratin. It's the same stuff that makes feathers and dinosaur claws.

Hair-raising hair

Here's your chance to hoodwink your hairdresser with a few hair-raising facts.

1 Most people have about 100,000 hairs on their heads. Fair-haired people can have 150,000 and red-haired people have to make do with about 90,000. (I wonder who counted them all!)

2 Hair grows at about 1 cm a month or 0.33 mm a day. Hot weather makes your hair grow faster. So if you lived at the North Pole you wouldn't need your hair cut so often – and you wouldn't want it cut so often.

3 Most hairs fall out before they reach 90 cm (35 inches) long. It's quite normal to lose up to 60 hairs a day. Any more than that and you might start going bald!

4 Hair is horribly strong. One hair is stronger than a copper wire of the same thickness. A rope made from 1,000 hairs could lift a well-built man.

5 Your hair stands on end when you're scared because little muscles in the skin pull on the roots of the hairs. The aim is to make you look big and fearsome to an enemy. That's why cats fluff their fur when they're going to have a fight!

GOSH – HE LOOKS BIG AND FEARSOME!

Nail-biting notes

Now mystify your manicurist with these nails' tales.

1 Your nails grow from an area underneath the skin called the nail bed. (This is nothing to do with the bed of nails that Indian fakirs sometimes sleep on.)

2 If you trap a nail in the door it will stop growing and drop off. With a bit of luck a lovely brand new nail will grow underneath. That's OK then!

3 Sometimes toenails start burrowing into the surrounding flesh. This horribly hurtful condition is caused by not cutting the nail straight across. But cutting nails is better than biting them!

4 Nail biting doesn't exactly kill you – but it looks revolting and makes your nails sore, and it helps lots of germs leap into your mouth. It also tends to put people off their soup in posh restaurants. Especially when you chew your toenails as well!

5 If you didn't cut your nails for a year they would be 2.5 cm (one inch) long.

But that's nothing compared to some people!

Record-breakers

Longest finger nails Shridhar Chillal of Pune Maharashtra in India stopped cutting his finger nails in

1952. By 1995 the nails on his left hand had reached 574 cm (226 inches) long.

Longest hair Mata Jagdamba of India has hair 4.23 m long. This is amazing because, as we've already said, normally a hair will stop growing and drop out by the time it reaches 90 cm (35 inches).

Longest beard Hans N. Langseth of the USA grew a 533 cm (209 inches) long beard. Sadly, Hans is no longer with us – he died in 1927. But you'll be relieved to know that the famous beard is now a museum exhibit.

PROPERTY OF MR H.N.LANGSETH

Longest moustache Kalyan Ramji Sain of Sudargarth, in India has been growing his moustache since 1976. In 1993 it was 339 cm (133 inches) wide.

Runner-up: A Briton, John Ray, started growing his moustache in 1939. By 1976 his moustache was 189 cm (74 inches) wide. But then he sat on one side of it in the bath and 42 cm (16 inches) of hair split off the end.

MY LIFE'S WORK'S JUST GONE DOWN THE PLUG HOLE!

Bet You Never Knew!
Even with hair all over it, your skin can sense things that touch it. Oh, so you DID know that! Well, bet you never knew that the human fingertips are so sensitive that they can feel an object move even if it only stirs a thousandth of a millimetre. Sounds like a really touchy subject! And touch is just ONE of your five sense-sational senses.

SENSATIONAL SENSES

Congratulations! You're a sensitive person – how could you be anything else with your super-sensitive touch, sight, taste, smell and hearing? And whether your view of the world is happy or sad, your senses help make sense of what's going on around you. But they're also horribly incredible in their own right – in fact they're SENSE-ATIONAL!

Sensitive senses quiz

Which senses are too sensationally sensitive to be true?

1 Your senses are so sensitive that they only take a quarter of a second to let you know when something is happening. TRUE/FALSE

2 Your eyes can tell the difference between eight million colours. TRUE/FALSE

3 Your eyes are 1,000 times more sensitive to light than the most light-sensitive film. TRUE/FALSE

4 Some people can see ultra-violet rays produced by the sun. TRUE/FALSE

5 Your tongue can taste a single drop of lemon juice even if it's mixed up with 129,000 drops of water. TRUE/FALSE

6 Your nose can detect a cheesy old pair of socks 200 metres (219 yards) away. TRUE/FALSE

7 Your ears can tell the difference between two sounds even if they are only ten-millionths of a second apart. TRUE/FALSE

8 Your ears can identify 1,500 levels of sound from high-pitched squeaks to deep booms. TRUE/FALSE

9 Some people can hear air whooshing around in the upper atmosphere. TRUE/FALSE

10 Your body can tell what time it is even if you're in a room without windows. TRUE/FALSE

Answers: 1 FALSE – your senses work much faster than that! **2** TRUE. **3** TRUE. **4** FALSE and don't try it. **5** TRUE. **6** FALSE – but I suppose it depends on how strong the socks pong! **7** TRUE – if the sounds come through separate ears. **8** TRUE. **9** Supposedly TRUE but unproven – half a mark for this answer! **10** TRUE.

Your touchy senses

You've heard about the sensitive sensors under your skin? Well, did you know that they too come in no less than FIVE sensational varieties? Each one keeps you in touch in a different way.

To show you how, we need a brave volunteer. Can you

35

spot which sensor is doing the sensing in the five tests below?

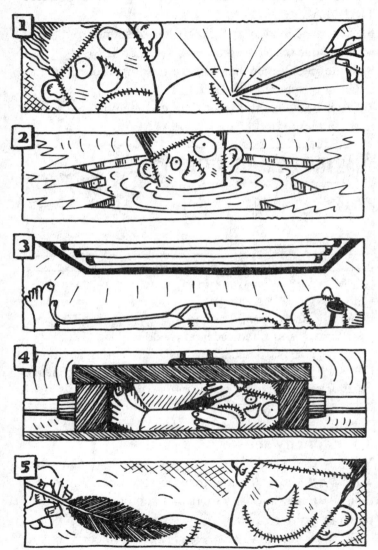

These are the sensors that you must match with the pictures. Some are named in honour of the scientists who discovered them. The person who discovered nerve endings deserves a special mention – it must have been a very painful experience.

a) Ruffini's receptors – for heat
b) Krause's receptors – cold
c) Nerve endings – pain
d) Meissner's receptors – touch
e) Pacinean receptors – pressure

Answers: 1 c) 2 b) 3 a) 4 e) 5 d)

Pain – good news and bad news!

You might think that the nerve endings that bring you painful feelings are only there for the nasty things in life. And you'd generally be right. But surely there's some good in everything?

The good news – 1
You have 500,000 sensors to keep you in touch with the outside world. Hooray!
The bad news – 1
And 2,800,000 nerve endings to make you painfully aware of any horrible aches and twinges. Boo! Hiss!

The good news – 2
But luckily your brain has its own built-in pain-killers called endorphins. This is why a soldier can lose a leg in battle and hop along without feeling any pain! Hurray!

The bad news – 2

Afterwards it hurts A LOT – and not only that. People who lose arms and legs often feel their missing limbs itching even when they're not there! Shame!

WHAT'S MAKING MY LEG ITCH DOC? – IT WAS CUT OFF THREE YEARS AGO!

WOODWORM!

The painful truth

Pain is there to warn us that we're getting hurt. "Stop!" say your nerve endings. "And try to be more careful next time!" It's a sensible message. So you see, a bit of pain is good for you! Sounds a bit like the sort of thing your teacher might say, doesn't it? But is that good news?

A sensational sight

Your most sensational sense is sight. After all, without it we'd all be in the dark! But did you know that your eyeballs are like tiny little video cameras full of watery jelly? Is this the sort of camera that you'd like to discover in your Christmas stocking?

The eyeball camera

Seeing really is believing with the incredible EYEBALL CAMERA. Now you can keep up with the speediest sporting action even at night! Just point your camera in the right direction. Wherever you go, your EYEBALL

CAMERA goes too! In fact, it's so useful it's worth you using the two that you've already got – you know, those gloopy blobs that sit snugly in your eyeball sockets!

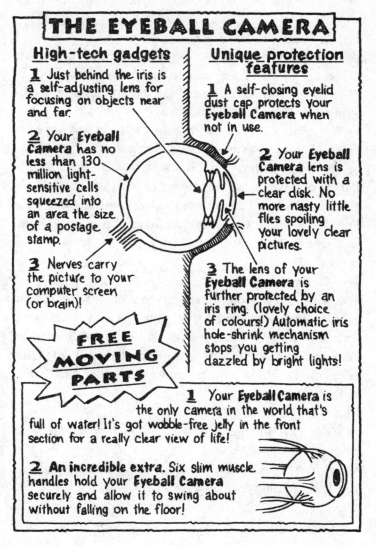

THE EYEBALL CAMERA

High-tech gadgets

1 Just behind the iris is a self-adjusting lens for focusing on objects near and far.

2 Your Eyeball Camera has no less than 130 million light-sensitive cells squeezed into an area the size of a postage stamp.

3 Nerves carry the picture to your computer screen (or brain)!

Unique protection features

1 A self-closing eyelid dust cap protects your Eyeball Camera when not in use.

2 Your Eyeball Camera lens is protected with a clear disk. No more nasty little flies spoiling your lovely clear pictures.

3 The lens of your Eyeball Camera is further protected by an iris ring. (lovely choice of colours!) Automatic iris hole-shrink mechanism stops you getting dazzled by bright lights!

FREE MOVING PARTS

1 Your Eyeball Camera is the only camera in the world that's full of water! It's got wobble-free jelly in the front section for a really clear view of life!

2 An incredible extra. Six slim muscle handles hold your Eyeball Camera securely and allow it to swing about without falling on the floor!

Dare you find out for yourself . . . how your eyeballs work?

Naturally you'll want to try out your sensational eyeball camera as soon as possible. So here are a few tests to try.

Test 1: Seeing in the dark

You will need a darkened room, a torch and a tomato. Shine the torch at the tomato and then away from it. What happens to the colour of the tomato as you shift the light away from it? Any idea why?

a) The tomato appears red both in the light and out of it. This is because the eye sees colour in the dark.

b) The tomato appears red in the light and grey out of it. This is because the eye can't see colours in the dark.

c) The tomato appears red in the light and blue out of it. This is because the dark confuses those little light-sensitive eyeball cells.

Test 2: Test your pupils*

You will need a darkened room and a mirror with a light over it. Wait in the room until your eyes are used to the dark. Cover your left eye with one hand and switch on the light over the mirror. Your uncovered pupil suddenly goes smaller. What's happened to your other pupil?

a) It's still large.

b) It's also gone small.

c) It's got even bigger.

* Or you might prefer to test your teacher's pupils – you'll be getting your own back!

Test 3: The vanishing eyeball mystery

Hold the book close to your face and close your left eye. Focus your right eye on the left eyeball. Now slowly move the book away from your face. Why does the right eyeball vanish?

a) The eye can't focus at a certain distance.
b) There's a gap in the light-sensitive cells.
c) The light-sensitive cells get tired and stop noticing things.

Caring for your eyeballs – eight things you should know

1 You don't need to care for your eyeballs at all! Your body does it all for you.

2 Eyeballs come complete with their own windscreen-washing service – it's called "crying".

3 Fortunately you don't have to be sad to cry. You can produce tears whilst being sick, coughing, or by getting something in your eye or, preferably by laughing!

TRAGIC – SHE ONLY WON THE <u>SECOND</u> PRIZE OF £10,000!

4 Tears are also spread over your eyeball when you blink. Every blink takes 0.3-0.4 seconds – that's half an hour each day, or five years of your life. What a blinking waste of time!

5 Any tears you don't use dry up in the drainage tube that leads from the corners of your eyes to the inside of your nose. These dried-up tears form the sleepy dust you rub from your eyes every morning!

6 Each of your eyes is protected by about 200 eyelashes. Each eyelash lasts three to five months before it falls out and another grows in its place.

7 Tiny mites live in the base of your eyelashes. They have eight legs each and look like alligators! But don't worry – they won't do you any harm. In fact they are doing you quite a favour by gobbling up harmful germs!

8 If, despite all this care and attention, your eyes don't see very well – you may need glasses.

Savage spectacles

One of the first people to wear "glasses" was the rotten old Roman Emperor Nero. He used a curved piece of emerald to help him enjoy the savage spectacle of lions tearing people apart at the Roman games. That sounds like really bad taste...

FAR OUT!

Terrible tastes and sickening smells

Here's the problem with taste and smell. They're sensational senses all right. They bring you some sensational sensations like your favourite foods and the smell of roses. But they also bring you foul bitter tastes and sickening stinks!

Terrible tastes

To find out more about taste you've got to peer into your

wet drooling mouth. Better take a look now before you chicken out!

Look closely at your tongue. Say Aghhhhhh! Can you see those little bumps and lines? The little lines are crammed with 8,000 or so taste buds linked to the brain by nerves. Different buds handle sweet, sour, salty and bitter tastes.

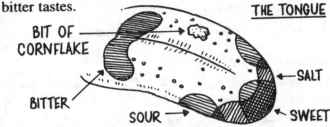

THE TONGUE

BIT OF CORNFLAKE

BITTER

SOUR

SALT

SWEET

The really tasteless question is – why are you supposed to taste bitter things at all? I mean – how many bitter-tasting foods do you actually like enough to eat? Well, you're not actually meant to eat most of them – spitting them out would be a lot better for you. This is because most poisons taste bitter, so the bitter-sensitive taste buds are there to tell you that you're just about to eat some vile POISON.

YOU WANT THE **BITTER** TRUTH? ...HE'S BEEN POISONED!

Sickening stinks

Your smelling equipment is a 2.5 cm-square patch in the top part of the area behind your nostrils. This patch has over 500 million tiny thread-like sticking-out bits called cilia (silly-ah).

Cilia have a really sickening job – they hang around in groups of eight from rod-like trunks buried in snot. (Yuck!) Smells take the form of tiny bits (called molecules) that float about in the air. When a smelly molecule lands on one of the cilia it triggers a chemical change that's passed on as a signal to the nerves.

Sensationally sensitive

Your sense of smell is sensationally sensitive. It's actually 10,000 times more sensitive than taste! That's OK when there's something nice to be sniffed but there are some really revolting odours around. And did you know your nose can sniff one molecule of the stinky juice squirted by a skunk even when it's mixed with 30,000,0000,000 molecules of fresh air?! Yeuch!

Bet you never knew!
People lump taste and smell together because. . .
1 They work together to help you appreciate the delicious flavour of your favourite foods.
2 In fact when you're eating your favourite fries and thinking, These are sensationally scrummy-tasting chips, *you're actually smelling them!*
3 If you couldn't smell them they'd probably taste like cardboard!
4 That's what happens when you have a snorting stinker of a cold. Your nose is blocked up by snot and because you can't smell, your food doesn't taste like it should! Sounds horrible!

Silly sound detectors

Ears are eerie things. After all, just think how odd some people's ears look. And guess what? They're even odder on the inside! Just listen to this. . .

How the ears work

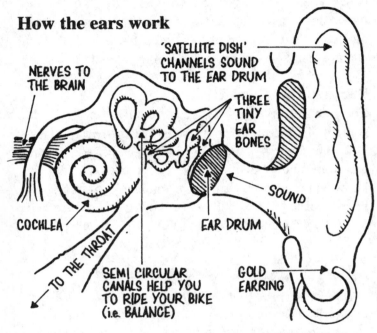

NERVES TO
THE BRAIN

'SATELLITE DISH'
CHANNELS SOUND
TO THE EAR DRUM

THREE
TINY
EAR
BONES

SOUND

COCHLEA

TO THE THROAT

EAR DRUM

SEMI CIRCULAR
CANALS HELP YOU
TO RIDE YOUR BIKE
(i.e. BALANCE)

GOLD
EARRING

The ears work like a couple of satellite dishes linked up to a drum, linked up to a triangle and stick linked up to a microphone with a carpenter's level attached! Simple, isn't it?

1 Like satellite dishes, your ears pick up signals in the air and bounce them into the central hole. With your ears, the signals in question are sounds.

2 The eardrum's a bit like a real drum. It trembles when sounds hit it.

3 The trembling eardrum makes the tiny ear bones jangle just like a triangle hit by a stick.

4 The cochlea picks up the sounds and makes them into nerve signals that go to the brain. It's a bit like a microphone picking up sounds and sending them down a wire.

5 Like a carpenter's level, the semi-circular canals are full of liquid that sloshes around as your head moves. Sensors in the canals stop you losing your balance. This is good news for tight-rope walkers!

An urgent horrible health warning

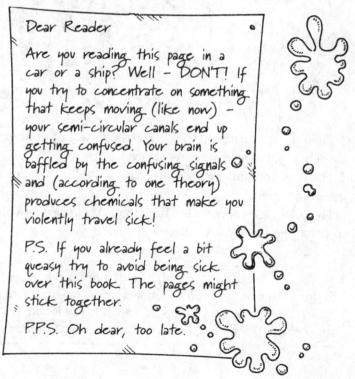

Dear Reader

Are you reading this page in a car or a ship? Well – DON'T! If you try to concentrate on something that keeps moving (like now) – your semi-circular canals end up getting confused. Your brain is baffled by the confusing signals and (according to one theory) produces chemicals that make you violently travel sick!

P.S. If you already feel a bit queasy try to avoid being sick over this book. The pages might stick together.

P.P.S. Oh dear, too late.

Dare you find out for yourself . . . why your ears go POP?

Try listening to yourself yawning. You may hear a few tiny tingling pops at the start of the yawn – keep trying if you don't hear them at first! So what causes them? Clue: it's something to do with your eustachian (you-station) tube – a useful little tunnel linking your mouth with the inner parts of each ear.

1 The tube is closing up to protect the insides of your ear from being yawned out of your head.
2 The tube contains little poppers that sound off when air goes past them.
3 The tube is opening up to allow the extra yawned-in air to reach the inside of your ear.

Answer: Normally the tube is closed but it opens if the air pressure increases at either end. Examples might include when you suddenly go down or up a steep hill or when you breathe in deeply.

Taking leave of your senses

Each one of your senses is unique and sensational in its own way. But they all have one thing in common. They all need someone or something to talk to and give them a quick answer. So they send all their information to the same place – your very baffling BRAIN.

THAT MAKES SENSE!

THE*BAFFLING*BRAIN*

Your brain is baffling. Baffling, bemusing, bewildering and brain-bogglingly bamboozling. For instance, how can this 1.5 kg (3 lbs) of pinkish-grey blob be more powerful than the most powerful computer in the entire known universe? Everything it does is baffling – including its mystifying memory and strange sleeping habits.

CLICK
BUZZ
WHIRR

WATKINS – WHAT IS 7693271 ÷ 15134?

508·34353 SIR!

What does the brain do all day?

Now there's a baffling question. Unlike other parts of the body it doesn't seem to do anything exciting like squirt blood, leap about or fight germs. It just sits there wobbling nervously. It looks like a watery blancmange and it even squelches if you poke a finger in it and waggle it about.

But the brain is always busy. Even when it doesn't seem to be doing much your brain is crackling with the electrical force of millions of nerves – just tell that to your teacher next time she accuses you of daydreaming! Your brain fires off signals, feelings, orders and thoughts at incredible speed. And in order to perform at such baffling speed your brain needs some strong nerves . . . lots of them.

Nerves fact file

Name of body part: Nerves

Where found: Form a network throughout the body but mainly in the spine and connecting to the brain

Useful things they do: Take info from your senses to your brain. Bring orders from your brain to the rest of your body.

Grisly details: You can wire a battery to nerves in a chopped-off finger and make it twitch. There's one for the school science lab!

Amazing features: Nerves can carry signals at 100 metres (109 yards) a second – that's one of their slower speeds!

Speedy signals

Nerve messages are electrical signals zipping down the nerve cells and leaping from cell to cell. Phew – sounds tiring! The nerve cells don't actually touch one another. Signals are passed on by chemicals that leap the gap between cells and spark an electrical pulse on the other side.

Reckless reflexes

Most of the signals from your nerves go to your brain to
tell it what's going on in the different parts of your body.
But some messages move so fast that they make you do
things before you realise it and control it. Sounds like a
good excuse for doing something really reckless – like
breaking things!

But if reflexes are moves you make without thinking,
which of these aren't reflexes?

1 Snatching a hand
away from the heat

2 Blinking

3 Riding a bicycle

4 Sneezing

5 Getting washed in the morning

6 Hair standing on end when scared

7 Rolling the eyes

8 Eating breakfast

Dare you find out for yourself . . . how to test your reflexes?

Have you been hit below the kneecap by a doctor wielding a small rubber hammer? If so – it was probably to test the nerves that cause a reflex that works when you're walking. Here's how to do it yourself.

1 Rest one leg loosely over the other.

2 Lightly tap the upper leg just below the kneecap. What happens next?

a) The leg jerks forwards.

b) The leg jerks backwards.

c) A small purple patch appears on the lower leg.

I SAID **SMALL RUBBER** HAMMER!!

Reflexes are alright as far as they go. But to do anything interesting you need to ask your baffling brain.

Baffling brain fact file

Name of body part: Brain

Where found: Inside the top part of your skull.

Useful things it does: Bosses the rest of your body about. In charge of your memories, thoughts, dreams, etc.

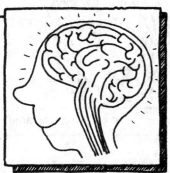

Grisly details: Your brain cells started dying off as soon as you were born. And they aren't getting replaced.*

Amazing features: The brain is more than 80 per cent water!

*Fortunately you've got 15,000 million cells up there ~ more than enough for a long life-time! That's:

- Three times more than a gorilla.
- Seven million times more than a stick insect.
- And about 900 million times more than a small worm that sometimes lives in the human gut.

Teacher's brain tour

If the brain is incredibly baffling on the outside – the inside is even more baffling. It's like a big office building (even your teacher's is quite big) with lots of rooms filled with people doing things you don't understand. Well, here's a guided tour of your teacher's office block – I mean – brain.

Note: Don't touch anything on the tour as it might give your teacher a brainstorm! And don't remove any of your teacher's brain cells either – he or she hasn't got enough to spare!

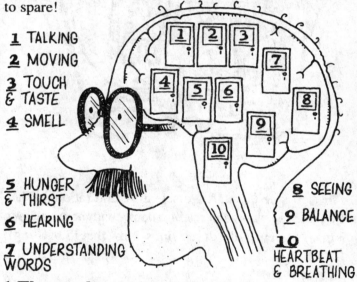

1 TALKING

2 MOVING

3 TOUCH & TASTE

4 SMELL

5 HUNGER & THIRST

6 HEARING

7 UNDERSTANDING WORDS

8 SEEING

9 BALANCE

10 HEARTBEAT & BREATHING

1 The cerebrum (ser-re-brum)

Includes your teacher's library where his or her murky memories are stored. Also the boss's office where decisions are made, and offices for the speech, hearing, moving, touch, sight, understanding and feelings (probably a very small office in this case) departments.

2 Two separate halves

Many of these offices are split into two halves linked by communication cables. In the right half the staff are artistic and emotional. They enjoy painting and arranging flowers.

In the left side the staff are scientific and rational. They enjoy playing chess and reading books with no pictures in them. (They even like doing sums. Now that IS baffling!)

3 Thalamus

This is the switchboard that relays information from all your senses to the brain.

4 Limbic (lim-bick) system

This is where your teacher's feelings are checked to make sure he or she can feel anger, fear, sadness – and even happiness. (Yes – teachers do occasionally experience this emotion.) The staff make sure your teacher doesn't get so happy he walks around with a silly great grin all day.

5 Cerebellum (serry-bell-um)
Staff here control your teacher's more skilful movements. OK – there aren't too many of these.

6 Under-brain
This is another switchboard for transferring news about reflexes happening elsewhere in your teacher's body.

7 Hypothalamus (hi-po-thal-a-muss)
In this broom cupboard are the controls for your teacher's sweating, growing, sleeping and waking, thirst and hunger control systems. There's also the control panel for the autonomic nervous system. It's a big job for a little office!

8 The pineal (pi-knee-al) body

No one knows what goes on here. Perhaps it's your teacher's time-control system. It may tell your teacher to wake up in the morning and to stay awake through your science lesson! No – DON'T reset these controls!

Be a brain scientist

Can you use your knowledge of how the brain works to predict the results of these baffling brain experiments?

Experiment 1 In the 19th century, French scientist Paul Broca weighed 292 male brains and 140 female brains. He concluded that on average female brains weighed 200 g (7 ounces) less than male brains. How would you explain this result?

a) Men are cleverer than women.

b) Boys are more big-headed than girls.

c) Men have bigger heads than women.

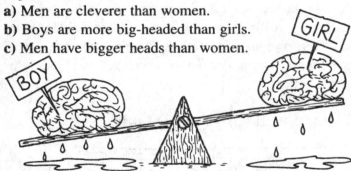

Experiment 2 In 1864, two French doctors were discussing what happens to the brain after the head is cut off. As luck would have it one of the doctors was due to have his head chopped off shortly. So the condemned doctor bravely agreed to try winking his right eye three times in response to a shout from his friend. But what was the result of this grisly experiment?

a) The head stuck its tongue out.

b) Nothing – because the brain was dead.
c) The head winked once.

WINK

HE DIDN'T SAY ANYTHING ABOUT OPENING HIS MOUTH!

Experiment 3 Some surgeons cut the nerves connecting the two halves of the cerebrum in order to combat brain disease. How do you think this affected the patients?
a) Each side of their body acted like a separate person.
b) They became twice as clever.
c) They died.

Dare you find out for yourself . . . how your friend's brain works?

Reassure your friend that this experiment does not

involve any pain. And they won't need to have their head cut off either. Absolutely not. But you do need to remember some rather baffling information.

• The left side of your vision is linked to the right side of the brain and vice-versa.

• The left side of the cerebrum is the half that imagines where to find something.

• The right side deals with maths questions.

1 Write down five or more baffling maths questions.

2 And write another list of five or more baffling requests to give directions from one place to another, e.g. from home to school.

3 Don't tell your friend the aim of the experiment. Stand facing them about three paces away.

4 Ask your friend a maths question followed by a whereabouts question until you have completed both lists.

5 Watch their eye movements. What happens?

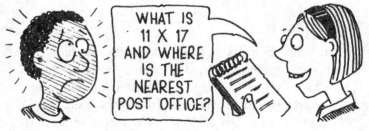

WHAT IS 11 X 17 AND WHERE IS THE NEAREST POST OFFICE?

a) Their eyes roll upward before they answer the whereabouts questions and go cross-eyed with the maths questions.

b) Their eyes go right for the maths questions and left for the whereabouts questions.

c) Their eyes go left for the maths questions and right for the whereabouts questions.

How to baffle your teacher

Here's how to baffle your maths teacher with your amazing brain power.

1 Ask your maths teacher the answer to the sum 4 divided by 47. Try to sound rather casual as if you've just thought up the question.

2 Make sure your teacher doesn't cheat by using a calculator.

3 After a lengthy pause for thought your teacher should be able to come up with something like 0.08 or even 0.085.

4 Smile sweetly and say,

"I don't think that's quite right. I think it's 0.08 510638297872340425531914893617021276594468."

5 Pause to savour the expression of shock on your teacher's face.

6 Hopefully your teacher won't realise that this incredible feat of mental arithmetic has already been performed by Professor A.C. Aitken of Edinburgh University.

7 Of course, if you don't happen to be a mathematical genius you'll have to learn the answer off by heart. (Tip: it's easier if you learn the numbers in groups of three or four and then string them together.)

Baffling learning

One of the most baffling things your brain does is

learning. It's incredible how they expect you to learn so much. Children at school have to learn on average TEN new words every day! But that's nothing! For example, Bhanddanta Vicittabi Vumsa of Burma learnt 16,000 pages of religious text off by heart.

Russian journalist Solomon Veniaminoff never forgot anything he learnt in his entire life!

Learning is all about remembering things. But the really baffling thing about learning is that scientists don't quite understand how memory works! Or maybe they can but they can't remember. But it's thought to involve electrical and then chemical changes within the brain cells. Or something like that. It's all very vague . . . and very baffling.

The baffled brain

The baffling brain is easily baffled. Just take a look at the picture below – is it a vase or are they two heads? See what I mean? Your brain just can't make up its mind.

No laughing matter

Chemicals such as pain-killers can also baffle the brain. Some just deaden pain without knocking you out, but the more powerful pain-killers actually cause the brain to lose consciousness. So who invented these powerful drugs? Well, it's a painful story.

Once upon a time surgeons performed operations without any pain-killers. They would cut off your leg or whip out vital portions of your anatomy and all you got was a gag to stop you screaming too loudly! But that was before Mr Horace Wells got in on the act.

Connecticut, United States, 1844

Horace Wells was deeply in on the act. And he wished he wasn't. The act in question was a display showing the effects of laughing-gas and Horace was in the audience. But Horace Wells wasn't really watching the show at all because he was busy being in agony. The plump, smartly dressed dentist was suffering from the most embarrassing ailment for anyone in his profession . . . toothache. It was so annoying – that he, the great Horace Wells – the inventor of a wonderful new solder for fixing false teeth should have to endure this awful indignity.

He made another effort to concentrate on the entertainment. Laughing-gas, or nitrous oxide, as scientists called it had been discovered about 70 years before. And it didn't just make you laugh. A few whiffs had even the most outwardly boring person singing, dancing, fighting, talking nonsense or even passing out. The hugely popular laughing-gas shows employed bouncers to protect the audience from the crazy antics of volunteers who breathed the gas.

Suddenly, one of the volunteers went berserk. There was a struggle and the man got injured – but he didn't seem to feel any pain!

Lucky you, thought Horace Wells nursing his aching jaw. Then a little light bulb flashed inside his head and for the first time that evening he smiled. (Just a bit – you can't smile too easily with toothache.) If laughing-gas could deaden pain and knock you out . . . then perhaps . . . perhaps just maybe. . .

After the show Horace Wells approached the organiser with a somewhat baffling request.

"Could you lend me some laughing-gas?"

Wells hoped to knock himself out whilst another dentist removed the aching tooth. In those days pulling out a tooth was a painful and rather bloody job involving a huge pair of tongs and a great deal of tugging. But Horace Wells breathed in the gas and didn't feel a thing!

"It's a new era for tooth-pulling!" he exclaimed in triumph as the effects of the laughing-gas wore off. Or that's what he meant to say but since his mouth was still sore the words probably came out as,

ITCH AR HUGH HIERA FUR HOO-FARLIN!

Yes, he, Horace Wells was about to sell the pain-killing secret of laughing-gas and become rich and famous. Seriously rich.

But the pain-killing project came to a rather painful conclusion. The first public use of laughing-gas by a dentist ended in disaster when the patient woke too soon. He had received too little gas. During a later operation another patient died after receiving too much gas. A few years later Horace Wells himself came to a painful end. He went mad as a result of breathing too much pain-killing gas and in 1848 he took his own life. But he didn't die in vain. Today the idea of using a pain-killing gas (not laughing-gas!) for operations is well-established.

Fortunately you don't need to rely on gas to send you to sleep.

Your brain's baffling bedtime

Every night at about the same time your brain does something remarkable – and quite baffling. It winds down its operations, pulls down the shutters and more or less switches itself off. Yes, that's right, it goes to sleep. Altogether your brain will spend at least 20 years in this odd condition. Why? Well, the really baffling bit is that no one really knows!

HURRY UP – I WANT TO SWITCH OFF!

All you need to know about sleep – in three easy lessons

In order to make sleep less baffling here is a course of sleep lessons. It's taught at night school, of course, and unlike ordinary school, the teachers don't mind if you nod off!

Lesson 1 – falling asleep

1 Make sure you are neither too hot nor too cold. It helps if you go to bed at the same time each night.

2 Lie very still with your eyes closed. Try counting backwards from 1,000 or imagining yourself on a lovely relaxing holiday.

3 You'll notice that you can't pin-point the moment when you fall asleep. Some people feel they are falling and twitch violently at this point so they have to start all over again!

Lesson 2 – what happens when you're asleep?

1 Here are a few things you ought to know before you fall asleep. Whilst you are sleeping. . .

- Your body temperature starts falling.
- Your weight drops by 28-42 g (1-1.5 ounces) each hour.
- You can change position up to 40 times a night.
- You can wake up for less than three minutes at a time

and you probably won't remember it in the morning.

2 Don't worry about listening out for danger whilst you're asleep – your brain does this job automatically.

3 Here are some things you shouldn't do whilst asleep.

- Try not to sleep walk – about one in 20 children do this.
- Try not to snore too loudly. This disgusting din is made by someone sleeping on their back with their mouth open. As they breathe in, the wobbly bits at the back of their mouth start rattling noisily.

4 You can stop snorers by putting something hard and prickly (such as an old hair-brush or hedgehog) into the bed. The snorer rolls onto his back and the prickles wake him up!

5 After about 90 minutes of sleep your eyeballs start twitching but the nerves to most of your muscles shut down so you can't move. You are about to enter the most baffling part of your sleep – the DREAM ZONE.

Lesson 3 – exploring the dream zone

1 Welcome to a strange world where time and space have no meaning and where nothing is impossible.

2 Dreams are caused by signals fired towards your brain by nerves underneath it. When you are awake this area screens out boring sounds – that's why you don't notice

traffic or your teacher droning on and on and on.
Zzzzzzzzzz.

3 Most dreams take 6-10 minutes but the record for the longest dream is 150 minutes! During your 20 years asleep you can look forward to watching 300,000 dreams!

4 Every night you make several trips to the dream zone.

5 Some good and bad dream news. THE GOOD NEWS: Happy dreams are three times more common than sad dreams. THE BAD NEWS: As it gets towards morning you are more likely to encounter nightmares. If you're reading this in bed you'd better save the next chapter till morning – you don't want to dream about ghastly groaning skeletons now, do you?

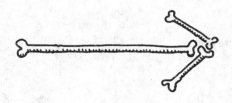

BONES {AND} GROANS

Bone up on bones

Spooky stories are full of groaning skeletons. But skeletons don't groan for the fun of it. No. They're groaning because that's what bones do to you. They ache and they break and if you happen to have muscles attached to your bones they ache even more! Funnily enough, bones make some scientists groan too. Well – imagine having to remember all 206 bones in the human body! Here are a few of the more memorable groans – er, I mean bones.

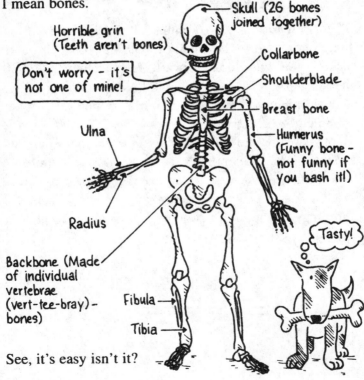

Horrible grin
(Teeth aren't bones)

Don't worry – it's not one of mine!

Skull (26 bones joined together)

Collarbone

Shoulderblade

Breast bone

Humerus
(Funny bone – not funny if you bash it!)

Ulna

Radius

Backbone (Made of individual vertebrae (vert-tee-bray) – bones)

Fibula

Tibia

Tasty!

See, it's easy isn't it?

70

Bones fact file

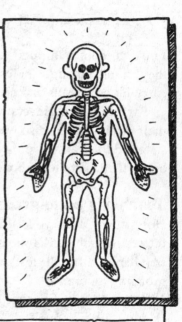

Name of body part: Bones

Where found: Your bones form the skeleton that makes up about 25 per cent of your weight. Bones are made from a tough stringy substance called collagen (collar-gen), and strengthened with a mixture of hard materials.

Useful things they do: They hold your body upright and give your muscles something to pull against.

Grisly details: If you took all the minerals out of your thigh bone you could tie what's left in a knot.

Amazing features: A broken bone repairs itself. As long as the broken ends are "set" or put back together - new bone grows over the break.

Bones – the inside story!

Some bones are solid with an area of spongy bone on the inside, others are long and hollow and their empty centres are filled with juicy jelly-like red marrow. Dogs love marrow because it's full of meaty goodness. So should you. Your marvellous marrow makes you 173 BILLION brand new blood cells every day.

Look at bones through a microscope and you'll see they've all got little holes in them. These tiny tunnels carry blood vessels and nerves.

They're called Haversian canals (Have-er-shun) after their oddly-named discoverer – Clopton Havers. It may seem odd to call these tiny tubes "canals" but it sounds better than ' Clopton's bone-holes" at least.

Teacher's bone-groan test

How much does your teacher really know about this interesting subject? Bone up on the answers to this ultra-fiendishly difficult test and show up your teacher's groaning ignorance!

1 You will only find one of these bones in the human skeleton. Which one?

a) The tail bone

b) The elbow bone

c) The nose bone

2 If you wanted to hold up a heavy weight what would be the strongest thing to use?

a) A stone pillar

b) A concrete pillar

c) A leg bone

3 A giraffe has seven bones in its neck. How many neck bones has a human got?

a) 3

b) 7

c) 12

4 How many bones does a baby have?

a) 206, just like a grown-up person.

b) 86

c) More than 350

5 Some Tibetan priests use the skull as a drinking cup. How much liquid do these creepy cups hold?

a) 500 ml

b) 1.5 litres

c) None – it trickles out through the eye-sockets.

6 What bone forms the sticking-out bit of your ankle?

a) The bottom of the tibia

b) The ankle bone

c) The top of the heel bone

7 What is a wormian bone?

a) A wiggley little bone in the little toe.

b) An extra bone sometimes found in a baby's skull.

c) A bone infested by worms.

Answers: 1 a) Yes – that's right! We've all got tails! The coccyx (cox-sicks) is a mass of three to five joined-up bones at the end of the backbone. Fortunately it's not long enough to poke outside the body! **2 c) 3 b)** The giraffe bones are much longer! **4 c)** Lots of these extra bones join up as the baby grows up. **5 b) 6 a) 7 b)**

73

What your teacher's score means:

0-3 Make no bones about it – your teacher is a bone-head!

4-5 Your teacher can teach you a few facts but only knows the bare bones of the subject.

6-7 Your teacher is probably an osteologist* (ost-tee-ol-o-gist). He or she may even have a real human skeleton at home for study purposes.

* An expert on bones.

Bet You Never Knew!
An osteologist studies bones looking for clues that can identify the person to whom the skeleton belonged. Do you think you could do this? Here's your chance to use your skills to solve a truly horrible true mystery.

The wandering bones

It was 7 December 1976, Long Beach, California. The TV cameraman was in for a nasty shock. He was in a haunted house side-show filming a TV series. As he moved a gruesome dummy away from the rest of the film crew – its arm fell off! The arm was real. And there was bone underneath!

The police were called but it soon became clear that this was no ordinary dummy – it had once been alive! The police discovered three fiendish facts. The body had been pickled in the deadly poison arsenic. It had been shot by an old-fashioned type of bullet dating from before 1914. In the body's mouth was a coin dated 1924.

The police then traced a series of former owners of the

body. The former owners (who had all thought the body was a dummy) were colourful showmen who scraped a living exhibiting the gruesome specimen at funfairs. The oldest showman thought he could remember buying the body in Oklahoma. Then local history buffs dredged up a possible identity for the butchered body – Elmer McCurdy, cowboy and outlaw.

Elmer McCurdy's luck had run out at dawn on 7 October 1911. When the sheriff's men came for him he was drunk with stolen whiskey and exhausted after a night spent hiding in a hayloft. A young lad was sent up to the hiding place.

"The boys want you to surrender, Mister!" he cried.

"I'll see them in hell first!" roared the outlaw.

McCurdy died with his boots on after slugging out a desperate gun battle until his six-gun was empty. After the outlaw's death an undertaker had preserved the body and charged people to see it propped against his parlour wall!

Many people tried to buy the body but all offers were refused. Then the undertaker gave the body away to a nice man who said he was Elmer's long-lost brother.

Three months later the body appeared in a street-show in Texas.

But could the police bone experts prove that the body actually belonged to McCurdy? Here is a description of the outlaw dating from 1911. Which of the following features might you be able to check by examining the bones inside the body?

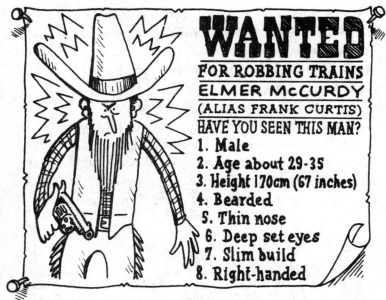

WANTED
FOR ROBBING TRAINS
ELMER McCURDY
(ALIAS FRANK CURTIS)
HAVE YOU SEEN THIS MAN?
1. Male
2. Age about 29-35
3. Height 170cm (67 inches)
4. Bearded
5. Thin nose
6. Deep set eyes
7. Slim build
8. Right-handed

Answers: 1 Yes, females have wider pelvic bones. **2** Yes, as he grew older some of his bones joined together. **3** Yes, by the length of the thigh bones. **4 5 6** No. **7** Yes, by looking at the build of the skeleton. **8** Yes, marks on the right arm bones showed traces of more developed muscles than on the left side.

After studying the bones the scientists were certain they

had the right man. The final proof came when they found
that an old photo of the outlaw's head perfectly matched
the shape of the skull. And so, at long last, Elmer
McCurdy's body was given a decent burial – nearly 66
years after he was killed!

Join up the joints

Could you be a bone expert? If so you'd need to know
how to fit a skeleton together. The bones in a skeleton fit
together to form joints and the trick is to assemble the
joints correctly. But it's not easy – there are over 200
joints to join up!

Here are the main types of joints.

1 Hinge joint. Joints such as the
knee work like door hinges,
allowing the bones to move
backwards and forwards. But
they don't move so easily from
side to side.

2 Gliding joint. The ankle
bones can easily slide up and
down and from side to side.

3 Ball and socket joint. As the
name implies this is a ball and
socket that allows arm and
thigh bones to move in most
directions.

4 Swivel joint. This joint
allows the bone on top to
move up and down and from
side to side.

5 Saddle joint. The bone on top is like a jockey on a saddle. So it sways about and leans in all directions – without falling off!

Lucky ligaments

Imagine if your arm fell off every time you threw a ball! This doesn't happen because tough cords called ligaments hold your bones together over the joint. Contortionists stretch their ligaments as they bend their bodies into horrible positions. You'd groan if you tried this! But did you know that your ligaments and joints allow you to scratch every part of your body? This is lucky if you don't have anyone to scratch your back. Try scratching your own back some time – but NOT during Science class.

OVER A BIT, DOWN A BIT. OOOH YES, THAT'S GOT IT!

Juicy joints

Your joints are surprisingly quiet. They don't groan – they don't even squeak. You can tiptoe softly because every major joint is cushioned in a bag of squelchy liquid. The liquid allows the joint to move smoothly and the ends of the bones are also padded with a softer material called cartilage (karta-lidge). The same stuff forms the bridge of your nose – but if you saw it in a chicken bone you'd call it "gristle".

Moaning muscles

No matter how supple your joints are – you can't make a move without using your muscles. THE GOOD NEWS is that you've got over 600 of them. THE BAD NEWS is that they can make you moan in aching agony!

Groaning muscles fact file

Name of body part: Muscles

Where found: Under the skin and surrounding various body bits.

Useful things they do: They're ALWAYS hard at work squeezing the food through your guts, pumping blood and so on.

Grisly details: Muscles can squeeze so strongly that they break your bones! But they have sensors to stop them squeezing that much!

Amazing features: Muscles are anchored to bones by tough tendons. A tendon won't go Twaang! unless you hang a 58-tonne weight from it!

Getting to grips with muscles

To get to grips with your muscles you need to take a closer look. A much closer look. . .

If you cut a muscle in half you can see that it's made of thick bundles of stringy fibres.

Look more closely and you'll see that a fibre is made up of smaller fibres called fibrils.

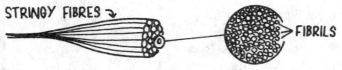

How to make a move

1 Ask one of your nerves to send a signal to your muscles. Make sure that the tiny fibrils are shortening in response.

2 Check that your blood contains enough sugars to provide the energy to power the muscle.

3 The muscle contains chemicals that produce energy by breaking up the molecules of sugar.

But before you move a muscle there are few more things you should know. . .

Groaning muscle facts

1 Muscles have complicated, instantly forgettable Latin names. See if you can remember these.

a) Gluteus maximus – bottom. Makes a nice cushion for sitting on.

b) Digital flexor – wags your finger at people.

c) Levator labii superior – helps you to snarl. Just say the word and you'll be snarling!

2 Muscles can pull but they can't push. That's why muscles work in pairs. One muscle pulls one way and the other muscle pulls in the opposite direction!

3 You can watch the tendons pulling your muscles. Just spread your fingers and waggle them up and down.

4 When you stick your tongue out there's no muscle doing the pushing from behind. A muscle pulls across the tongue and this pushes the tongue forward.

5 As people get older tough stretchy fibres build up inside the muscles. That's why giants and monsters don't like eating stringy old grandparents. They prefer a succulent tender CHILD! Help!

Groans at the gym

Well, be honest, how far can you run? Or does exercise – any kind of effort – make you groan? Are you one of those people who prefer lazing around on the sofa with a big bag of popcorn? Well, if so, you'll be pleased to hear that exercise can be BAD for you! Every sport should carry a Government Health Warning.

Horrible Health Warning 1 Getting off the sofa is dangerous! Your heart suddenly has to pump blood up to your brain and not along a level. Sometimes your brain doesn't get enough blood and you feel dizzy. That's why aircraft pilots sometimes faint on a sudden turn.

I WISH YOU WOULDN'T DO THAT CAPTAIN!

Horrible Health Warning 2 Even when you're up-and-running it's horribly hard work for your body. Your poor feet and ankles have to put up with a pressure of SIX times your body weight. The arches of your feet flop down as they hit the ground. Your fat wobbles, your brain squelches and even your eyeballs bounce slightly in their sockets!

FLOP   SQUELCH   WOBBLE   BOUNCE

Horrible Health Warning 3 Violent exercise is especially bad for you . . . it can cause some especially groan-worthy pains.

a) If your heart beats more than 175 beats a minute it could get injured... Slow down gently!

b) Stiffness. May be caused by loss of water due to sweating and build-up of a chemical called lactic acid in tired muscles . . . Slow down gently after exercise and enjoy a long drink.

c) Cramp is when your muscles squeeze painfully and you can't stop them . . . Keep the muscle warm and rest it. A nice hot-water -bottle will do!

d) Stitch. Caused by cold and running on a full stomach . . . Keep warm. Don't guzzle so much!

I PREFERRED BEING A COUCH POTATO!

But if there's one thing worse than taking exercise it's NOT taking exercise. Look what you miss out on.

HEALTHY GLOW! HEALTHY GLOW!

1) Having a strong healthy heart for pumping blood to every nook and cranny of your body.

2) A strong set of breathing muscles. They stop you from getting puffed out and help you cough up germs that try to sneak down your throat.

3) Keeping your joints supple and building up your staying power so you can enjoy the day without a single groan! And you can even build up a good appetite for a delicious dinner. Well, better eat now. After the next two chapters you may not feel quite so hungry.

‐DISGUSTING DIGESTION‑

Could you murder a rich chocolate cake dripping with cream and icing? Does the hint of jam roly-poly and extra-thick custard make your tummy thunder? If so – you're going to find this chapter horribly tasteless. Imagine your food being chewed and squashed and squelched as it's taken into your body. It's all due to your disgusting digestive juices.

Disgusting digestive glands

A gland is a body bit that produces juices. At different points in your guts, glands lurk – just waiting to spray your food with digestive juices. But can you believe the horribly huge amounts of juice they produce? We're not talking little squirts here. . .

Glands	Daily Squirt
Saliva	2 litres *
Stomach	1-2 litres
Pancreas	1-1.5 litres
Liver	1 litre

That's a total of over six litres every day!

* You end up gulping most of this down! Yes, that's 50,000 litres (5,500 gallons) of spit in a lifetime! Or enough to fill 100 baths!

Digestive juices contain chemicals called enzymes. The enzymes work horribly hard to break up the food molecules into smaller molecules that your body can absorb more easily. The hotter the body gets the faster these changes happen, until at 60°C they suddenly stop. Mind you, if you ever got that hot you'd be cooked anyway!

Dare you find out for yourself . . . how enzymes work?

Rennet is a sloppy substance that contains rennin – an enzyme also found in the human stomach. Make sure it's OK for you to use the ingredients below and get someone to help you use the hob.

852 millilitres (1.5 pints) of fresh full cream milk
Sugar
Rennet – available from supermarkets
Saucepan
Bowl
Tablespoon

1 Heat the milk in the saucepan and stir well until it's warm but not hot. DON'T BOIL IT!
2 Pour the milk into the bowl and stir in one tablespoon of sugar.

3 Place the bowl in a warm place.
4 Very gently stir in one tablespoon of rennet. Don't touch the bowl for ten minutes.

5 Ten minutes later . . . what's happened to the milk?

HORRIBLE HINT: If your experiment has worked, the rennin will have digested the milk.

a) It's turned into a disgusting smelly yellow mixture with soggy white lumps in it.

b) It's turned into a solid wobbly mass.

c) Nothing

A horribly healthy diet

Are you a fussy eater? Your body is! To stay healthy your body has to digest a balanced diet. That means all the types of food shown below and NOT just the ones you like!

1 Fibre helps your guts grip your food and keep it moving on its long trek to the toilet.

2 Proteins help your body build and repair its cells. Ten per cent of your body is made of this stuff.

3 Carbohydrates (car-bo-hi-drates) are found in starchy foods. Once they're digested they become sugars that your cells turn into energy.

4 Sugars provide your body with easy energy. Your lazy body feeds the sugars straight to the cells.

5 Fat is a useful store of energy and it helps build body cells – often in a wobbly layer around your tummy.

A sickening sandwich

Could you combine foods that contain fibre, proteins, carbohydrates, sugars and fat in a ONE sandwich snack?

HAM AND JAM SANDWICH

Here are some possibilities.

1 A ham and jam sandwich with a fizzy drink.

2 An egg and baked beans wholemeal-bread sandwich (yuck!) and a mug of hot chocolate.

3 A chip sandwich with white bread followed by treacle pudding washed down with loads of lemonade (burp!).

4 A healthy wholemeal lettuce sandwich followed by a sugar-free nut bar and a glass of mineral water.

A horribly unhealthy diet

As if digestion isn't horrible enough just look at the horribly unhealthy things that some people eat.

1 Some people eat earth. This is horribly unhealthy because it's teeming with germs and tastes disgusting.

2 In 1927 a woman complained of stomach pains. She was rushed to hospital in Ontario, Canada. There, doctors found that she'd swallowed 2,533 objects including 947 bent pins.

I'VE GOT PINS AND NEEDLES IN MY STOMACH!

X-RAY VIEW

3 But the prize for the most disgusting diet must go to Michel Lotito of France. In his own country he is known as Monsieur Mangetout (Mr Eat-it-all). Since 1966 Mr Eat-it-all has chomped his way through. . .

89

He generally eats 900 g (31 ounces) of metal a day. All without getting indigestion. (Don't try this yourself – you might not be so lucky!)

4 The urge to eat is controlled by the hypothalamus in the brain. It tells you when you are hungry and when you are full. A scientist removed part of a rat's hypothalamus and it gorged itself until it was a horribly unhealthy fat rat.

5 At this moment millions of people are trying to lose weight by dieting. But people don't actually need to lose weight unless they are horribly unhealthy. Like William J. Cobb, for example.

In 1962 William J. Cobb weighed 364 kg (57 stone). He was so round that he could only roll like a barrel. Not surprising – considering he was carrying 91 kg (14 stone) of fat! So William decided to go on a diet and within a year or two he was down to 106 kg (16 stone, 7 lbs). He had lost the weight of three large men!

LARGE BAR OF CHOCCY

HEALTHY STICK OF CELERY

BEFORE

AFTER

6 Most people can only lose about half their normal body weight. This takes about three weeks if the person doesn't eat. Then they die – and that's a really unhealthy thing to happen!

Horribly healthy diet complications

To stay horribly healthy you need more than a balanced diet. You've got to eat things that you can't see or taste – like minerals for example. Luckily you don't have to go around looking for minerals to eat. Ordinary food contains minerals in tiny amounts – and that's all your body needs! For example, slurp a milk shake and you're doing your bones a favour. Milk contains the bone-building minerals calcium and phosphate. Then there are other chemicals called vitamins and they're really VITAL.

Vital vitamins

Vitamins are vital because if you don't get enough of them in your diet you become horribly unhealthy. Feel more like gobbling up those greens now?

Vitamin	Found in:	Not enough causes:
A	Milk, butter, eggs, fish oil, liver.	Lots of illnesses and you can't even see in the dark.
B1 and 9 other B vits.	Yeast and wholemeal bread. Also found in milk, nuts and fresh vegetables.	Victim loses energy and can't get out of bed – sounds worse than a Monday morning.
C	Oranges and lemons. Fresh fruit and vegetables.	Loss of teeth, bleeding gums, dark spots on body. Bad breath. Yuck!
D	Oily fish, dairy products.	Bent bones and bandy legs. Bad news for footballers.
E	Wholewheat bread, brown rice and butter.	Scientists aren't quite sure about this one.
K	Green veg, liver	Blood doesn't clot properly – very messy!

It took scientists a great deal of trial and error to discover the disgusting effects of lack of vitamins. But solving these medical mysteries gave them something to crow about.

The sick chickens mystery

Eijkman Christianson was at his wit's end.

In 1884 he had gone to Indonesia to study a mystery disease. The locals called it, "I can't."

He injected animals with germs thought to cause the disease. The animals stayed healthy!

Then his pet chickens went down with the disease.

He moved them to another place and they got better!
But why?

Maybe they just needed some fresh air.

Or maybe it was due to a change in diet? In their first
home the birds were eating boiled rice.

Now they were eating brown rice.

It turned out that the brown outer layer of the rice
grains was rich in Vitamin B. This prevented, "I can't"
or as we call it, beri-beri.

Mind you, it took Eijkman many years of experiments to prove that eating the wrong rice had made the chickens sick. As for the chickens themselves – things could have been worse. Imagine if something had gone wrong with their digestive bits and pieces. They'd have been sick as parrots then! Yes, we're talking about the gruesome guts!

THE *GRUESOME* GUTS

Guts are gruesome. Gobsmackingly, grossly, stomach-churningly sickening. In fact – if you thought too much about where your food went you wouldn't feel like eating it! But if there's one thing even more gruesome than guts, it's the scientists who find guts fascinating. Oh yes, and then there's the smelly stuff that pours out the other end. Yuck!

Gruesome guts fact file

Name of body part: Guts

Where found: Mostly under the chest area in the lower part of the body. (See below.)

Useful things they do: Absorb your food once it has been digested.

Grisly details: The guts form a continuous tube up to 8m (8·7 yards) long. That's longer than a huge slithery snake!

Amazing features: Your guts are held in place by the mesentery (mes-en-terry). This stops the guts slopping about and tying themselves in knots!

Dare you find out for yourself . . . what's inside your mouth?

Open wide! Here's where it all begins. The gobbling, munching mouth – grinding up the goodies before they hit the guts. Imagine what it's like to be a bit of food!

Tooth truths

The first thing you'll have to worry about are those gigantic spit-dripping jaws. They're made from enamel and they're so tough you need a diamond to drill into them. Inside each tooth there are nerves and blood vessels just like any body part. Not all teeth are the same – there are different-shaped teeth for different jobs. Here are a few that we picked up from a dentist's floor.

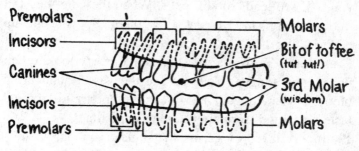

So how many teeth have you got? It depends on how old you are. You started off with 20 teeth that appeared when you were very young. As you get older these fall out and new teeth push through your gums. Here are some tooth totals – which is closest to your own number of teeth?

1 Incisors   a) 2   b) 8   c) 4

2 Canines   a) 2   b) 4   c) 8

3 Pre-molars a) 4   b) 8   c) 12

4 Molars   a) 4   b) 8   c) 12

Answers: 1 b) 2 b) 3 b) or c) Younger children have four pre-molar teeth and adults have eight. **4 b)** or c) Younger children have eight molar teeth but adults often have 12.

Can you spot any of these in your mouth?

Uvula (You've-yer-la) This horrible little wobbly bit spends its time hanging around in your mouth. The name means "little grape" – can you see why? No one knows exactly why it's there but it does help you swallow.

Mouth lining If you look at this through a microscope you will see loads of soft cells. When they die they fall into your spit and you swallow them. So you end up eating yourself!

Frenulum (Fren-u-lum) This is the nasty-looking bit under your tongue. You can see the vessels that bring blood to your tongue and give it the energy to talk and taste your food (sometimes at the same time!).

Plaque A layer of germs that cluster on our teeth – they're responsible for tooth decay and bad breath! (If you find any, brush it off!)

Gruesome gobbling

Once you've checked your mouth – get ready to swallow. Oddly enough most of us manage to do this without thinking. This is probably because swallowing is a reflex action. But it's also a horribly complex operation – see if you can do it by following these instructions. (NOTE: try not to dribble all over your nice clean book.)

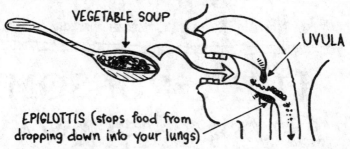

VEGETABLE SOUP

UVULA

EPIGLOTTIS (stops food from dropping down into your lungs)

1 Using your tongue press some food you chewed earlier on to the roof of your mouth.

2 Force the food towards the back of your throat.

3 Swing up your uvula to prevent the food making a dash for freedom up your nose. On second thoughts don't worry about doing this – it happens automatically.

• NOTE 1: Try not to laugh when you eat. When you laugh your uvula swings DOWN – so you could find that the soup you've just slurped up is dribbling out of your nostrils!

• NOTE 2: Try not to breathe whilst you're swallowing. If you do your food goes down your windpipe and you have to cough it up! You've got a little lid called the epiglottis (eppy-glot-tis) that closes off the top of your windpipe to prevent this happening.

Wouldn't you like to know what really happens to your food after you swallow it? No? Go on – it's REALLY horrible.

A gruesome guts tour

Here's a gruesomely thrilling alternative to the usual boring tourist trip. Just imagine being shrunk down to the size of a pinhead and boarding a coach the size of a pea. Then imagine going on a guided tour of someone else's guts! And guess what? Your dinner's thrown in! That's if you feel like eating any . . .

The Horrible Holiday Company proudly present...

THE GRUESOME GUTS GETAWAY!

EMBARK ON
THE TRIP OF
A LUNCHTIME.

THE SMALL PRINT
1. If you get digested and turned into a chemical soup it's not our fault - OK?
2. There will be **no** toilet stops until the end of the tour.

1.00 pm Enter the mouth. Fasten your safety belts and close the windows securely. It's wet outside and we're about to dive down the gullet waterfall. Splosh!

GRUESOME GUTS TOURS →

1.01 pm
Amazing 9 to 13-second free-fall as we're squeezed 25cm (10 inches) down the gullet!

1.02-6 pm Five hour stopover in the stomach. Plenty of time to admire the slimy stomach walls with their 35 million digestive juice-producing pits.

▶ Enjoy the beautiful sunset effect as a red hot pepper makes the stomach glow.

▶ Listen to the mighty roar of the rumbling stomach as trapped gases squelch around amongst the food.

▶ Experience the gut-churning thrill of the stomach big dipper as it churns and churns again every 20 seconds. (If you feel a bit queasy, sick-bags are provided.)

6.00 pm A sudden lurch takes us from the stomach into the intestine. Then what better than a relaxing 6m (6·5 yards) cruise down the scenic small intestine? (Speed 2·5cm (1 inch) per minute.)

▶ Feel the lovely smooth gliding motion as we're squeezed along. The slimy gut walls help to stop the guts from digesting themselves.

▶ Marvel at the velvety insides of the intestines made up of five million tiny projections called villi.

▶ Gasp as we are covered in enzyme-rich digestive juices squirting down from the pancreas and liver.

▶ Wonder as the food chemicals are sucked into the villi.

▶ Puzzle over the mystery of the appendix. Everyone's got one of these finger-like things sticking out of their intestines. But no-one knows what it's for!

10.00 pm Spend the night in the comfortable and spacious large intestines. Here the surroundings are peaceful, lie back and listen for the

relaxing gurgling of the water as it's taken out of the remains of the food and back into the body.

7.30 am (Give or take a few hours). Put on your life jacket and parachute. It's time for splash down in the toilet!

102

Some sickening scientists

Of course, the first scientists who investigated the guts had to learn the hard way. That's by gruesome guesswork, sickening speculation and some awful emetic* experiments.

* WARNING TO READERS: An emetic is something that makes you throw up. Vomiting is a reflex action caused by strong squeezing of the muscles around the stomach. It could even be triggered by reading this chapter. Don't try any of these experiments at home – or at school!

Emetic experiments

If you thought that science is all about spotless white coats and squeaky-clean labs . . . THINK AGAIN! Here are some sickening experiments you shouldn't try.

1 René Réamur (1683-1757)

Claim to fame: Famous French scientist. Expert on just about everything, including technology and industry.

Emetic experiment: Trained a kite – (that's a bird not the thing on a string) to sick up its food. Then he pored over the vile vomit to see what the half-digested food looked like.

Disgusting discovery: The meat didn't go rotten inside the bird's guts. This was because the chemicals in the bird's stomach killed the germs that made things rot.

MUST BE THAT RABBIT I CAUGHT LAST NIGHT!

2 Lazzaro Spallanzani (1729-1799)

Claim to fame: Famous Italian scientist. Expert on volcanoes, electric fish, thunderclouds and how a snail grows its head back after you cut it off.

Revolting research included:

o Forcing animals to swallow tubes of food and then making them sick so he could study how the food had changed. The animals included cats, dogs, oxen, newts, sheep, a horse and some sinister-looking snakes.

o Doing the same experiment on himself. Eating his own sicked-up food. He ate one bit of food three times just to see how it had changed!

o Making himself sick again so that he could study his own stomach juices.

Emetic experiment: Kept a container of sick in a warm place for a few hours.

Disgusting discovery: The food continued to be digested. (This was because the enzymes produced by the stomach didn't stop working.)

OH DEAR – IT MUST HAVE BEEN SOMETHING YOU ATE!

3 Claude Bernard (1813-1878)

Claim to fame: French scientist. Cut up loads of human bodies and made disgusting discoveries about blood and nerves.

Revolting research: Kidnapped dogs (or should this be "dognapped"?) for his experiments. Poked tubes into the poor pooches' stomachs to find out what was going on

Emetic experiment: Added juice from a dog's pancreas to fatty foods.

Disgusting discovery: The fats were digested and made a greasy mess. (This was because digestive juices produced by the pancreas digest fats.)

Could you perform experiments like these? Would you want to? If your answer is "YUGGGHHH!" or "WHICH WAY TO THE BATHROOM?!" then you don't have the stomach for the job. So you wouldn't want to be at Fort Mackinac, United States in 1822...

The stomach for the job

The young man moaned in agony. A carelessly loaded shotgun had exploded – blasting a 15 cm (6 inch) hole in Alexis St. Martin's side . . . you could see all his insides. The young Canadian hunter had two broken ribs, a damaged lung and . . . a hole in his stomach.

Dr William Beaumont looked at these injuries and shook his head sadly. The patient would die soon. Very soon. In those days the only treatment for this type of wound was to slap on a bandage and arrange the funeral. But against all expectations, Alexis survived the night. Weeks became months and the young man even started to get better! But he had an embarrassing problem.

The stomach hole refused to heal. So whenever he felt peckish Alexis had to bandage his tum to stop its gruesome contents from slopping out!

Oddly enough the young man cheerfully put up with this appalling arrangement. So the devious doctor seized the opportunity to perform some gruesome gut experiments. One day he asked Alexis to swallow a bit of raw meat on a thread. Later he pulled it up again to see how it had changed. On another occasion Dr Beaumont poked a thermometer through the hole and watched it leap about as the stomach churned!

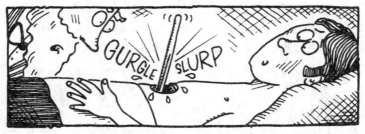

The doctor soon discovered that stomach juice is produced in large amounts when there's food in the stomach. So he drained some of Alexis's stomach juice out through a pipe and tried to identify the chemicals it contained. First of all he tasted it – YUCK! But as he wasn't sure what it was he sent it to some scientist friends.

They discovered the juice contained hydrochloric acid – a powerful dissolving chemical. This is useful for breaking down food and killing germs.

Sometimes the doctor and his patient would have a row. You've got to see it from Alexis' point of view. For two years Dr Beaumont had nursed him. But on the other hand . . . well, if there's one thing worse than having a hole in your body – it's being chased around by a meddlesome medic trying to terrorise your tummy. And over the next few years Dr Beaumont took to following Alexis so he could perform even more horrible experiments!

Oddly enough these shouting matches provided Dr Beaumont with yet more sickening scientific data. He couldn't help noticing that when Alexis got cross, his stomach went all red and quivery!

At last in 1833 Dr Beaumont published his findings. It had taken 11 years of tests and tantrums. Packed full of stomach-churning pictures, the book was an overnight success. The doctor achieved fame and fortune. Yet he owed his entire achievement to one gruesome fact . . . he'd had the stomach for the job!

A weighty matter

Three hundred years ago an Italian scientist named Santorio Sanctorius decided to build an incredible weighing machine. It swung from the ceiling and was big enough for his chair, desk and bed! There was even room for his prized silver chamber pot. Every day Santorio sat in the machine and recorded his weight.

For 30 years he weighed himself. He weighed himself before meals, after meals and during meals. He even weighed all his waste products.

But he still couldn't figure it out. Why did his food weigh more than the contents of his silver chamber pot?

Here's the answer. Much of the missing food turns into energy to power the body. Digested food molecules go from the guts to the blood and then off to feed billions of hungry body cells. Spare sugar and fats get carted off by a useful blood vessel to the storage place in the liver.

Liver fact file

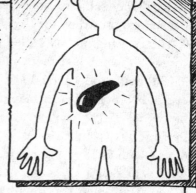

Name of body part: Liver

Where found: On top of the guts and under the diaphragm.

Useful things it does: What doesn't it do? (See below.)

Grisly details: If the liver doesn't work, waste body products build up in the skin.

Amazing features: You can lose 90 per cent of your liver and survive. That little bit of liver grows into a lovely new liver!

The lively liver

Yes – your liver certainly has a good time – scientists know of 500 jobs it tackles. There may be even more that haven't yet been discovered! The liver. . .

• Controls the amount of sugar in the blood. This is done with the aid of a substance called insulin produced by the pancreas. Too little insulin causes a disease called diabetes.

• Stores spare fat and carbohydrates.

• Makes Vitamin A.

• Gets rid of old red blood cells.

• Produces digestive juices.

• Keeps you warm – all these activities produce heat!

But not all your food is used by the body. Some of it just ·isn't needed – so the body chucks it out!

Gruesome garbage disposal 1 – waste food

1 Every day some of your food puts in a reappearance. It's stained brown by the liver's digestive juices – lovely.

2 This waste food is called faeces – that's Latin for "dregs" – which just about sums it up.

3 Children produce 65-171g (2-6 ounces) of the stuff every day. Some fearless scientists have discovered that faeces is 75 per cent water, and of the solid material that's left, two thirds of it is food that your body can't digest such as fibre, fruit skins and seeds. And the other third is made up of . . . germs!

4 Yes! Your guts swarm with billions of germs that have somehow managed to get past the acid in the stomach. Ugh! Fortunately, few of them do much harm.

5 UNFORTUNATELY, they do produce gases which, added to the gases from food and drink, can reappear at either end of the body – with hilarious or embarrassing but always noisy (and sometimes smelly) results.

6 But the really bad news is that these gases include methane, a chemical that burns easily. (NOTE: please don't experiment on yourself or your teacher to prove this. One surgeon cut open a man's guts and caused a gas explosion!)

Gruesome garbage disposal 2 – waste water

Much of your food is made up of water. Cucumbers, for example, are 90 per cent water and ten per cent vegetable. Your body is over two-thirds water and water is very useful for making lots of gruesome body fluids such as tears, runny snot and digestive juices. But spare water just isn't needed so it's filtered out by your kidneys.

Kidneys fact file

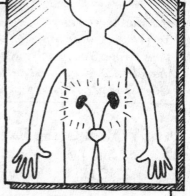

Name of body part: Kidneys

Where found: You've got two at the back of your body just below your lowest ribs.

Useful things it does: Remove spare water, unwanted salt and waste chemicals from the blood.

Grisly details: If not enough water passes through the kidneys the waste forms agonisingly painful stones.

Amazing features: Your kidneys filter 1 litre (1.76 pints) of blood every minute.

How the kidneys work

The kidneys are like millions of tiny coffee filters linked

up to a drainpipe.

1 Each filter takes the form of a tiny tube.

2 A little capsule at the start of each tube takes in fluid from the blood.

3 As the fluid runs down the tube, all the really useful stuff such as molecules of food escape back into the blood.

4 All the useless unwanted water plus any extra salts and poisonous wastes trickle down the drainpipe into the bladder.

5 This watery waste is urine.

Bet you never knew!
You can discover a person's state of health by studying their urine. Too much sugar in the urine is a sign of diabetes. Doctors used to taste urine to discover this! Disease may also cause a change in the colour of urine.

Are YOU a Urine Expert?

Can you link the colour of these urine samples to the disease? NOTE: feel free to colour in the urine yourself!

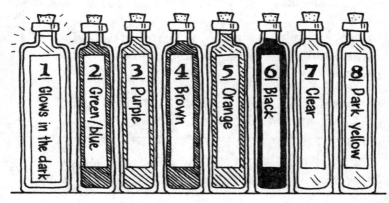

1) Glows in the dark
2) Green/blue
3) Purple
4) Brown
5) Orange
6) Black
7) Clear
8) Dark yellow

Cause of the colour. . .

a) The patient has been injected with blood from an animal.

b) Blackwater fever – a nasty tropical disease.

c) Cholera or typhus (both deadly diseases).

d) The patient has been drinking a lot of liquid.

e) The patient has been eating too much beetroot or blackberries.

f) The patient is feverish and has lost a lot of water by sweating.

g) The patient has been eating a high protein diet.

h) The patient is a space monster.

Answers: 1 h) 2 c) 3 e) 4 b) 5 f) 6 a) 7 d) 8 g)

Of course, your kidneys couldn't work if your blood wasn't doing its job. That's rushing round your body as fast as your heaving heart can pump it out! Warning. If the sight of buckets of blood makes you wobble at the knees it's wise to put on a blindfold before reading the next chapter.

THE BL**OO**DY BITS

You may think that EVERYTHING to do with the body is blood-curdling. But some bits are bloodier than others. Take, for example, blood itself and the heart that keeps it moving. But blood is also vital for life – here's why. . .

Blood fact file

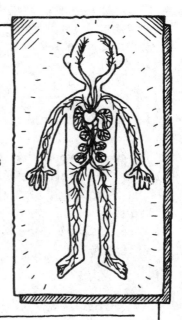

Name of body part: Blood

Where found: Throughout the body in a network of blood vessels. You've got about five litres of the red stuff.

Useful things it does: Delivers food and oxygen and other useful things your cells need to keep going.

Grisly details: You can lose one third of your blood without harm. But if you lose half – it's FATAL!

Amazing features: Blood is so full of things that it's amazing they all fit in – see below.

Blood – what's in it for me?

1 Your blood is yellow! Yes, it's true. If you leave a test tube full of blood for a few hours the blood cells sink to the bottom and you're left with a clear yellow fluid.

2 The yellow stuff is called plasma – it's 90 per cent water and 10 per cent chemicals such as those tasty molecules and minerals that your cells need to grow and stay healthy. Scientists have discovered how to dry plasma to a powder and turn it back into a liquid by adding water.

DRIED PLASMA

NEW PLASMA JUST ADD WATER! REFRESHES THE PARTS ORDINARY BLOOD CAN'T REACH!

BEFORE   AFTER

3 Imagine blood as a sort of hot soup squirting through your body. It's full of sugars and other molecules from your food – which is why vampires and mosquitoes find it so tasty.

AND IT ISN'T TOMATO SOUP!

4 Blood is thicker than water. In fact, it's THREE TIMES thicker. That's not surprising considering that blood is swarming with cells . . . here's what you get in one teeny little millimetre-sized drop!

- 7,000 white blood cells
- 500,000 platelets – (these are little bits of bone-marrow cell that help your blood to clot).

- 5 million red blood cells

Impressive isn't it? But that's nothing. . .

5 In all, your body contains. . .

- 35,000,000,000 (35,000 million) white cells,
- 500,000,000,000 (500,000 million) platelets and
- 25,000,000,000,000,000 (25 trillion) red blood cells.

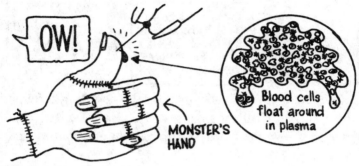

OW!

MONSTER'S HAND

Blood cells float around in plasma

Or so the scientists say. . .

6 But this is only guess-work because it's impossible to count all those cells.

7 The problem isn't just the huge numbers. Every second, three million new red blood cells are made in your bone marrow and three million others die. So by the time you've finally finished counting – you've got to start all over again!

8 There's plenty of room for all these blood cells. Your body contains about 96,558 km (59,962 miles) of blood vessels. If you took someone's blood vessels and laid them end to end they'd go twice round the world. Just imagine a motorway like that!

But if you want to zoom along the blood superhighway in your very own nippy little red blood cell you'll have to learn the rules of the road.

The blood Highway Code

RULE 1: Understand the one way system. Arteries go <u>AWAY</u> from the heart and veins go <u>TOWARDS</u> the heart. <u>NOT THE OTHER WAY ROUND!</u>

RULE 2: No "U" turns allowed. Valves in the veins form bottle necks that stop you reversing.

RULE 3: Red blood cells travel in the centre and white cells creep along the edges.

RULE 4: Make sure you can identify these other road users.

RED BLOOD CELLS   WHITE BLOOD CELLS   PLATELETS

RULE 5: Make sure you don't go over the speed limits. In the big arteries over the heart it's one metre every two seconds. In the capillaries — that's the very tiny blood vessels — it's one metre every half-an-hour!

RULE 6: After four months all the red blood cells must report to the liver scrap yard to be broken up. All platelets to be broken up after two weeks.

RULE 7: Beware of blood clots around wounds! All the platelets stick together and produce chemicals that make the plasma sticky. Other road users steer clear — unless you're a real clot!

If you ever get a bit short of blood you might need a blood transfusion. That's when you're given someone else's blood instead of your own. Luckily you don't have to give it back.

A blood-curdling story

Three centuries ago scientists began to wonder whether it was possible to inject blood into humans. But would it work? There was only one way to find out!

One day in 1667 an audience of top British scientists gathered to watch a terrifying trial transfusion. At the centre of attention was a man who had bravely volunteered to have an extra 340 g (12 ounces) of blood injected into his veins. The red stuff had been kindly donated by – a sheep!

1 Can you guess what happened?

a) The volunteer survived.

b) The volunteer's hair turned woolly and he died.

c) The volunteer went mad.

Answer: c) He was described as a bit "cracked in the head". But the scientists reckoned the test worth repeating and more blood transfusions were performed.

But then disaster struck. A man died after another blood transfusion in France. No one knew why! The doctor who performed the operation was accused of murder and although he was found not guilty, the French government banned all transfusions.

Meanwhile the Brits carried on. In those days the technology was rather primitive. One day a doctor offered a sick old man the chance of a blood transfusion. Here's what the doctor planned to do. . .

- Fix a silver pipe to each end of a length of chicken gut.
- Wash the chicken gut out with warm water.
- Stick one silver pipe in the arm of a healthy volunteer.
- Stick the other pipe in the old man's veins.
- Allow the blood to flow into the old man.

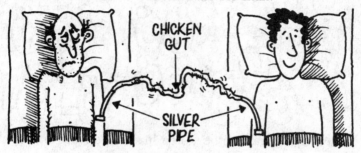

CHICKEN GUT

SILVER PIPE

2 What do you think happened next?

a) The old man said "YUCK – NOT ON YOUR LIFE!" and died soon afterwards.

b) The old man said "YES" but the transfusion bumped him off.

c) The old man said "YES" – he got better but the volunteer died!

Answer: a)

During a transfusion there was a risk of blood clots forming and blocking vital blood vessels. But what caused these killer clots? The answer emerged in 1900 when Austrian scientist, Karl Landsteiner, discovered that blood was divided into groups. Your blood group depends on the type of chemicals carried by your red blood cells. When red blood cells from different blood groups collide they mistake one another for germs! Germ-zapping chemicals on the outside of each cell zip into action and the cells end up glued together.

Nowadays blood can be stored in a blood bank until it's needed by someone with the same group. Blood banks don't save money but they do save lives. But sadly Karl's was not one of them. In 1943 he died of a heart attack caused by . . . a blood clot.

Oddly enough, whilst some doctors were trying to give their patients extra blood, others were trying to take it away again. These doctors thought that too much blood was bad for you.

Blood-thirsty bleeders

Yes – 200 years ago your local friendly doctor would do more than give you nasty cough medicine! He'd also try to open your veins to remove all that nasty bad blood! In those days doctors had a selection of vicious-looking knives especially designed for this gruesome job.

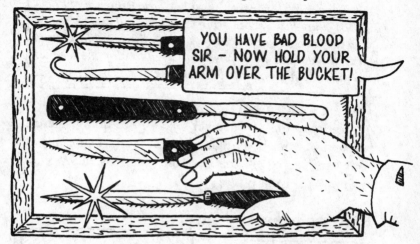

So you don't like the look of them? Well, don't worry – you do have another choice. Can you guess what it is?

A rotten riddle

What's green and yellow and dripping with slime, got ten stomachs, has three stabbing teeth at the front end and by the time it's finished with you it's 15 cm (6 inches) long and GORGED WITH ALL YOUR BLOOD?!

Answer: It's a LOATHSOME leech!!!

And here's the really BAD news! Surgeons were particularly keen on using leeches to take blood from children. They reckoned it was kinder than cutting the kids with the knives!

Bet you never knew!
French doctor, Francois-Joseph-Victor Broussais (1772-1838), thought leeches were lovely. In all it's reckoned that his leeches sucked 20-30 million litres of blood from his patients. The potty physician used to plop the leeches on his cringing patients 50 at a time.

The heaving heart

As you read this – whatever else you're doing, there's one part of your body that's hard at work. Especially if you were scared by that last bit. Yes, it's lucky your heart's in the right place.

Heaving heart fact file

Name of body part: Heart

Where found: The top of your heart is about 8cm (3 inches) to the left of your breast bone.

Useful things it does: Keeps your blood moving.

Grisly details: Your heart isn't heart-shaped – it's blob-shaped with a tangle of blood vessels on top. It's about 12cm (5 inches) high and weighs 250-300g (9-10 ounces).

Amazing features: It's horribly hard-working (see opposite page).

The horribly hard-working heart

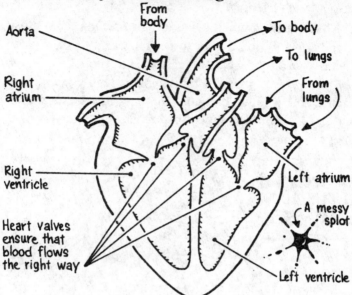

Aorta

From body

To body

To lungs

From lungs

Right atrium

Right ventricle

Left atrium

A messy splot

Heart valves ensure that blood flows the right way

Left ventricle

• Your heart is strong enough to pump blood round your body in one minute.

• Its speed is controlled by the brain and influenced by your feelings – this is why your heart beats faster before a science test. But the heart itself is powered by a built-in pacemaker that triggers the heartbeat with tiny electric shocks. So it's got to keep going!

• In just one day your heart pumps enough blood to fill a 10,000 litre (2,200 gallon) tanker.

• In an average lifetime it beats 4,000,000,000 times.

• And pumps over 300 million litres of blood. That's enough to fill 5,500 large swimming pools!

• And in all that time your heart doesn't stop once, not even when you're asleep.

Dare you find out for yourself . . . how your heart beats?

You will need yourself, a good pair of ears and a close friend. (If you don't want to get too close to your close friend you might want to get a plastic funnel too.) Just put your ear or funnel against your friend's heart. You should hear a sound that goes lup-dub, lup-dub, lup-dub, and so on. The "lup" should be louder and slightly longer than the "dub".

CAN YOU MAKE IT BEAT LOUDER PLEASE?

Look at the heart diagram on page 121. Each of the four chambers pumps blood in the direction shown. The "lup" sound is the valves at the opening of the ventricles slamming shut. Then the ventricles squeeze the blood out and the "dub" sound you can hear is the closing of the heart valves to prevent the blood squirting backwards.

Your heart isn't the only part of your body that beats. You can feel the blood pulsing in places such as the side of your wrist just under your thumb and on the sides of your neck. What causes these pulses?

a) The arteries pumping the blood forward.

b) The arteries bulging out as a surge of blood from the heart passes by.

c) A bulge in the veins caused by the blood stopping for a moment.

You might wonder why half your heart is squirting blood to your lungs. Well, your lungs are more than a couple of wheezy wind-bags. They're needed to supply your body with oxygen and the blood takes the oxygen round your body. And without this gas you'd be gasping!

THE GASPING LUNGS

You need your lungs like a breath of fresh air. Literally. Day after day, year after year, your lungs keep puffing away – about 600 million puffs in a lifetime. And you never need to remind them to do their job. But it's a difficult job and the facts that follow about breathing will leave you gasping.

Gasping lungs fact file

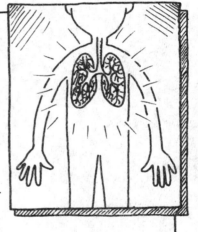

Name of body part: Lungs

Where found: In the chest on either side of the heart. The heart fits into a snug little hollow against the left lung.

Useful things they do: Breathe in air so that oxygen can get into your blood and supply your cells.

Grisly details: Once smokers get ash into their lungs they NEVER get it out again. Heavy smokers' lungs end up like tacky old tar buckets.

Amazing features: Your lungs contain 750 million little tubes and capsules. If these were laid out flat they could cover a tennis court.

Breathing: the inside story

"As easy as breathing" – or so they say. But in fact there's nothing easy about breathing. Here's what happens when you try.

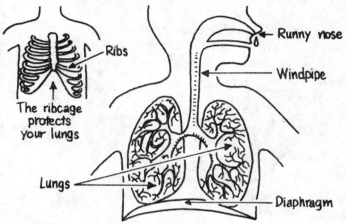

Ribs

Runny nose

Windpipe

The ribcage protects your lungs

Lungs

Diaphragm

1 Diaphragm (dia-fram) pulls down.
2 Your rib cage rises up.
3 Air is breathed in through your nose and mouth.
4 The air ends up in little capsules called alveoli (al-ve-ol-i).

Your breathing space

The alveoli are the places where breathing actually takes place. Oxygen gas from the air passes into the blood and hops aboard red blood cells for a free ride round the body. Meanwhile the carbon dioxide gas (produced as a waste product by your cells and dissolved in the blood) is rushing the other way. All this takes just one third of a second. Then, the breathing steps 1-4 go into reverse as the air is puffed out again. Yes, it all happens with breathless speed.

WHO'S FAKING THEIR NOBILITY?

Test your teacher

Is your teacher full of hot air? This tricky test will leave him or her breathless. Here's a clue to start him or her off. An adult breathes about six litres of air a minute.

1 A man stands in a telephone box to make a phone call. The telephone box contains about 270 litres (59 gallons) of air and once the door is closed no more air can get in. How long can the man speak on the phone before he faints from lack of air?

a) 45 minutes

b) 4 hours

c) 45 hours

2 A woman goes to sleep in a room 1.8 x 1.8 x 1.5 metres (2 x 2 x 1.5 yards). The room contains about 1,300 litres (286 gallons) of air. Would she have enough air to survive the night? (Clue: you only need about half the normal amount of air when you're asleep.)

a) Yes – and the following day too!

b) No – she'd die of suffocation.

c) Yes – just about!

3 Think about the size of the room in question 2. How much air do you need to last a lifetime?

a) Enough to fill two large airships.

b) Enough to fill a small hot-air balloon.

c) Enough to fill 339,174 hot-air balloons.

4 Why would someone die if they tried to hide in a lake and breathe through a hollow reed?

a) The lungs can't work in very cold water.

b) The water pressing against the body stops the lungs from breathing out.

c) The water gets in though the ears and drowning follows.

5 A woman has an attack of hiccuping. What part of her breathing equipment is making her hiccup?

a) Her diaphragm

b) Her ribs

c) Her lungs

WHO CARES? – I JUST WANT THEM TO STOP!

Horrible hiccups

What do you think caused this dramatic cure?

a) A massive electric shock

b) A faith healer

c) She had an operation

Dare you find out for yourself . . . how you talk?

TALKING. Some people never seem to stop. This sad affliction is particularly common amongst teachers. Naturally YOU know how to talk (and when to stop). But can you say what part your lungs play?

Half-way up your windpipe is a triangular opening. It's behind the little bump in your throat that some people call the "Adam's apple". On two sides of this opening, folds of skin stretch as you speak and wobble as air puffs past from the lungs. They're your vocal chords. The larger the chords, the deeper the sounds you can make (this is why most children have squeaky voices).

The basic sounds produced by your vibrating vocal chords are altered by the position of your tongue, lower lip and jaw. You can see how important these bits are when you try this unspeakable speech challenge.

1 Say the word "she" whilst keeping your tongue in your cheek (so you can't move it!).

2 Say the word "pie" without your lips touching one another.

STOP DRIBBLING!

3 Put your hand under your chin and try to talk without your lower jaw moving down.

DON'T WORRY IF YOU LOOK AND SOUND LIKE A JIBBERING IDIOT!

Which of the above were. . .
a) Possible
b) Just possible but it sounded funny.
c) Impossible
Enjoy endless fun watching your friends attempt the same challenge!

Answers: 1 b) 2 c) 3 b)

Gasping lungs sound-effects
Here are a few other sounds your gasping lungs can make. . .

Yawning
This happens when not enough air is getting to your lungs. So you suddenly take a deep gulp of air. It can also be triggered by boring science lessons.

Laughing

This happens when deep breaths, caused by movements of the diaphragm, are followed by a few short puffs of air from your lungs. This can be triggered by watching your teacher fall off his bicycle.

Crying

Your breathing is exactly the same as when you laugh. Only your feelings are different. Crying may occur as a direct result of having laughed at the wrong moment.

HA HA HA HEE HEE HO HO HO

YOU CAN STAY BEHIND AND MEND MY BIKE WATKINS!

But whatever you do with your lungs there is something you ought to know first. And it's no laughing matter . . . here's the bad news.

Breathing is bad for you

The air you breathe isn't always as pure as it could be. Especially if you live in a big city. Yes – every day you breathe in 20,000,000,000 (20,000 million) tiny bits of pollution, dust and dirt! THE GOOD NEWS . . . your body has ways of dealing with unwelcome visitors.

1 Inside your nose, windpipe and lung tubes there are tiny hairs called cilia (silly-er). Their job is to waft all that nasty stuff back into your mouth and nostrils.

2 The snot in your nose and windpipe is a deadly dust trap. Once stuck in the snot there's no escape for the

grimy gatecrashers. Have you ever noticed that when you work in a dirty place your snot turns black?!

The better news

You can actually cough up dirt . . . this involves closing the top of your windpipe and then suddenly releasing it to allow a blast of puff out at the speed of 150 metres (164 yards) a second!

And sneeze out snot. . . Something tickles the inside of your nose. You close and then open your throat. The air trapped in your lungs blasts its way out. Your tongue blocks the way into your mouth so the dirty, snotty mini-hurricane shoots out of your nose at over 160 km (99 miles) an hour!

ATCHOOOOO!

The really bad news

It's not just dirt and debris that make you cough and sneeze. The air we breathe is laden with billions and billions of germs. And their whole aim in life is to invade your body and cause disgusting diseases! Atishoooooooo!

YES, THE NEXT CHAPTER IS DEAD INTERESTING . . .

DEADLY DISEASES

Remember that sneeze at the end of the previous chapter? It was more than just a puff of air. It was a million droplets of snotty spit and countless germs zooming through the air in search of a victim. And causing disgusting or even deadly diseases. So welcome to the war zone right inside your body! Amazingly, most of the time you don't even know a war's going on!

Little monsters

There are thousands of different types of germs but they fall into two main groups. The brutal bacteria and the vicious viruses – but they're all little monsters.

Brutal bacteria

Bacteria come in a variety of sinister shapes and sizes. Some look like octopuses, others are like sausages and others still have little whip-like tails so they can swim around. They double their numbers every 20 minutes and increase their numbers eight times in one hour. In eight hours a single bacterium can make 16 million copies of itself!

There's something nasty in the garden shed. Something dark and invisible hiding in the corners of your school. And it's waiting to pounce. Many bacteria lurk in shadows because they're destroyed by sunlight. In gloomy weather they float on the wind as high as the clouds. And some are armed with poisonous toxins 100,000 times more powerful than the deadly poison strychnine!

Rogue's gallery

The brutal bacteria include microbes that cause boils, tetanus and upset stomachs. Vicious viruses include colds, chickenpox and measles. There are hundreds of other disease-causing germs – these are just a few of the more sinister specimens!

Botulinus (Bot-tu-line-us)

HABITS: Lurks in half-cooked potted meat, soil and rotting leaves.

DAMAGE REPORT: Deadly toxins. Cause double vision, sickness and death!

KNOWN CRIMES: Killed eight fishermen in Scotland in 1922. They had all eaten botulinus-infected sandwiches.

DANGER RATING: Deadly. It makes school dinners look healthy. (But don't worry, this disease is extremely rare!)

Leprosy

HABITS: You can only catch it from prolonged contact with people who already have the disease (and not everyone with leprosy has the catching sort anyway). Slow to develop. It can take years but in the worst cases it makes fingers and toes drop off.

DAMAGE REPORT: Attacks the nerves and skin.

KNOWN CRIMES: Affects several million people in hot countries.

DANGER RATING: Not so dangerous because it's difficult to catch - but very, very nasty if you've got it!

Vicious viruses

To a virus one of your body cells looks like a
little planet. That's not surprising because
viruses are thousands of times smaller even than
bacteria. The virus touches down onto a body
cell like a spacecraft landing on the moon. Then
the vicious virus injects chemicals to make the
cell produce hundreds more viruses. Within
half-an-hour all the viruses fly off to seek
more victims and the poor old cell splits like a
pea pod. It's died from over-work!

Influenza

<u>HABITS</u>: Changes its form every
year so your body's defences
can't recognise it easily.

<u>DAMAGE REPORT</u>: Fever, aches and
pains, runny nose - a few days
off school.

<u>KNOWN CRIMES</u>: In 1918 a world-wide 'flu epidemic
killed 25 million people.

<u>DANGER RATING</u>: No known cure. Luckily most types of
influenza don't kill you - otherwise you'd need
more than a few days off school.

Typhus

<u>HABITS</u>: Lives inside lice that
scratch their disgusting droppings
into the human skin. Ugh!

<u>DAMAGE REPORT</u>: Causes a red rash,
fever and death. Kills the louse
too by the way - but who cares?

<u>KNOWN CRIMES</u>: Unlike most criminals, typhus germs
actually enjoy prison. In 1750 infected lice
jumped from criminals to the judges and jurors at
a London trial. Three judges and eight jurymen
suffered the death penalty.

<u>DANGER RATING</u>: Still common in many parts of the
world but can be treated by drugs.

The body strikes back

Now for the good news. Your body is ready and waiting to bash germs – even if you're not! As part of its defences your body makes lots of germ-killing chemicals. How was this discovered? Well, the story's a bit of a weepie.

A tearful story

1. In 1921, scientist Alexander Fleming was breeding germs for an experiment. He had a bad cold. A drop of snot splashed the germs and they all died!

2. Fleming realised that snot must contain a germ-killing chemical. He experimented using blood plasma, spit and tears.

3. Tears were good germ killers. To get more, Fleming ambushed visitors to his lab and squirted lemon juice in their eyes! (Don't try this – it stings!)

4. He even picked on small children. (He paid them afterwards.)

5. Further experiments proved that egg-white also killed germs. So Fleming started breaking eggs.

6. Then he discovered that fish eggs killed germs too. So he went fishing – oddly enough this was his hobby!

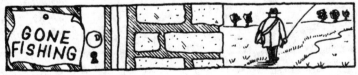

A rotten result

In 1965 scientists found that the germ-killing substance was an enzyme called lysozyme (lie-so-zime). It's found in all the things that Fleming tested. That's the good news. But sadly, lysozyme doesn't kill all known germs – just a few of them.

Luckily you've got a built-in army to defend you from germs. Every day they fight and die on your behalf. Recognise them? They're your wonderful white blood cells – all 35,000,000,000 (35,000 million) of them! Here's what they do.

Immune system fact file

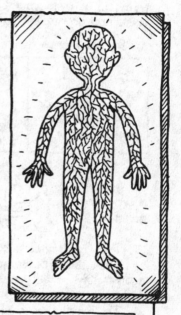

Name of body part: The immune system

Where found: A network of drainage tubes called the lymph system. Also includes your white blood cells.

Useful things they do: Fight germs and keep you healthy.

Grisly details: Pus from an infected wound consists of millions of white blood cells that have been done to death by germs.

Amazing features: White blood cells "talk" to one another using chemical substances that pass on messages such as, "Bash that virus!"

1 The tubes form a drainage system for lymph – a watery fluid that dribbles from the blood vessels.
2 Nodes: These grape-sized little lumps filter out nasty

germs from the tubes. They swell up and get bigger when you're sick.

3 Spleen: Helps make white blood cells in babies.

4 Thymus makes some white blood cells.

Your battling body

Here's how your body fights back. Germs are always trying to get into your body – through your nose, in your food or through cuts and scratches.

1. But your brave white blood cells are ready . . .

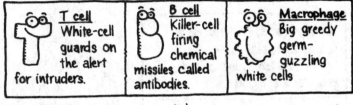

| T cell White-cell guards on the alert for intruders. | B cell Killer-cell firing chemical missiles called antibodies. | Macrophage Big greedy germ-guzzling white cells |

2. The T cell grabs a wriggling germ!

3. The T cell finds a B cell that makes antibodies that can stick this type of germ together. It's a desperate race against time – the germs are breeding fast!

4. The B cell fires antibodies to gum the germs together.

5. The T cell orders the B cell to make loads of copies of itself to attack any other germs loitering nearby.

6. The macrophage flows round the stuck-up germs. Reaches out long jelly-like arms to encircle them. Then it gobbles the germs! It can grab and guzzle 20 bacteria at a time and dissolve them whilst they're still alive! Congratulations, you win!

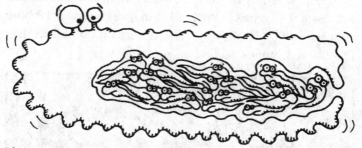

You've won if you destroy all the germs without losing too many white blood cells. It's OK to lose a few hundred thousand but lose a few billion and you're in trouble! Meanwhile bits of half-digested bacteria are left lying around on the battlefield.

How to be incredibly immune

Once you've had a certain illness, you needn't worry about getting it again – ever. Some of your white blood cells store the information about how to make the antibodies. This way, your body can store details of an incredible 18 billion types of antibody.

But sometimes your immune system needs a boost. That's why you need nasty injections. When you have a jab you are being injected with dead germs. YUCK!

These allow your body to make the antibodies needed to fight the actual full-blown disease. Yuck! This painful process is called vaccination. Here's how the modern form of vaccination was developed in 1796.

Just the jab

Some of the audience yawned rudely or snorted angrily. One muttered under his breath, "That Jenner's going on about cowpox again!"

These days few of the Medical Club members listened to the stocky figure in the buckskin breeches and the blue coat with yellow buttons. They'd heard it all before. But Dr Edward Jenner carried on regardless.

"Smallpox kills millions of people. It causes fever and covers the body with pus-filled spots. People lucky enough to survive are scarred for life. I believe that those who get the milder disease of cowpox are protected from getting smallpox."

"Why don't you experiment?!" someone shouted.

"Yes," yelled another, "On yourself!"

"But," shouted Jenner above the uproar, "many country people also believe it to be true!"

The audience exploded with laughter – they didn't think much of country folk.

Jenner sat back down – humiliated once again. He remembered going to the doctor's as an eight-year-old boy. He was terrified of the physician and the huge needle with its thread dripping with pus from a smallpox victim. This was the traditional form of vaccination using live germs and it was very dangerous. The needle scratch was supposed to cause a mild smallpox and somehow prevent the full-blown disease. But it gave young Jenner such a terrible fever that he nearly died.

There had to be a better way. Jenner was certain that people who got cowpox from milking infected cows never got smallpox. If only he could prove it. . .

One day, a young milkmaid named Sara Nelmes came into the tiny garden hut that Jenner used as his surgery. The girl was in a bad way.

She'd scratched her hand and as the doctor examined her he noticed bluish raised-up spots.

"You have the cowpox, Sara?"

"Yes, sir," the milkmaid blushed. "But at least I won't get the smallpox."

Jenner smiled. "Sara, with your permission I would like to perform a small experiment."

With a needle Dr Jenner took a drop of pus from Sara's hand and then. . . This was the moment for which he had waited for over 20 years. He decided to inject the pus into an eight-year-old boy named James Phipps. Then Jenner saw the fear in the child's eyes and remembered his own terror of the doctor with the huge needle.

So Jenner closed his eyes and gritted his teeth as he made two scratches on the boy's arm. In the next few days James would suffer the sores and discomfort of cowpox. But would this be enough to ward off the more deadly threat of smallpox?

Six weeks later Jenner held his breath as he scratched poor James again – this time with pus from a smallpox victim. Now came the real test. There would be a two week pause and then . . . what? Perhaps the boy would suffer crippling backaches, the fever and shivering and the deadly killer spots. Supposing Jenner was wrong . . . the child might even die. And then the doctor would face the death penalty for murdering his young patient!

But weeks passed and James remained healthy. The child was now immune to smallpox. Some people still jeered. They sang songs about people turning into cows after a cowpox injection.

"On their foreheads, o horrible crumpled horns bud;
Tom with his tail, and poor William all hairy . . ."

But Dr Jenner soon hit back with a book packed with tasteful colour pictures of pus-filled cowpox blisters. More physicians backed the doctor and soon richer people began to ask for the treatment. It proved to be "just the jab" for beating smallpox. Dr Jenner grew rich and successful but he never forgot the boy who had made it possible. What did he give James as a thank-you present?

a) His very own thatched cottage with flowers round the door.

b) A needle made from solid gold.

c) One shilling (that's equivalent to 5p).

Answer: a)

Smallpox smashed

The virus that caused smallpox was living on borrowed time. Throughout Europe and North America governments began to organise vaccination programmes. By 1980 a determined world-wide campaign of vaccination led to a historic announcement from the World Health Organisation . . . smallpox had been wiped off the face of the Earth. Meanwhile, scientists had discovered vaccines for many more diseases. In 1994 all British kids were given measles jabs. Ouch!

But even if you manage to remain healthy your body never stays the same. There's always something going on even if it's a bit of a pain. Oh well – it's all part of growing up.

GROWING PAINS

You might not always like your body – but it'll grow on you. You were growing even before you were born and you spend your first 20 years getting bigger. Growing is a bit of a pain for your parents because you always need new clothes and shoes. But after you stop growing you start ageing – and that's even more of a pain!

Relatively painful

Some of the biggest growing pains are caused by stupid comments from your relatives. Every Christmas they burst into your home to inspect you from head to toe and exclaim, "Haven't you grown!" At this point the best thing to do is look rather sad and say. . .

HAVEN'T YOU SHRUNK?

On second thoughts – better keep quiet or you won't get any presents. Here are a few things you need to know about growing.

Tall stories

1 You don't grow at the same speed all the time. You grow quickly in your first two years. Then up to the age of ten your growth steadies before speeding up again in your teenage years.

2 As you grow the proportions of your body change. For example, a baby's head takes up about 25 per cent of its length. But in an adult the head is only 12.5 per cent of its body length.

3 It's lucky these things happen otherwise you'd look pretty odd. You wouldn't want a giant-sized head – would you?

But why do people grow? If you asked a scientist this interesting question you wouldn't just get one answer – you'd get two!

1 The fairly simple answer.

2 The excruciatingly complicated but fascinating answer involving large dollops of scientific gobbledy-gook.

So which do you want to hear first?

THE HUMAN STRUCTURE ENLARGES WHEN TRIGGERED BY CHROMOSOMAL AND HORMONAL CHANGES, BLAH, BLAH, BLAH . . .

The fairly simple answer

The speed at which you grow is affected by diet. Eat a normal balanced amount of food and you'll grow taller than if you lived off scraps that the pigs won't eat. (No, I'm not talking about school dinners!) Health is also an important factor. Some bone diseases stop people from growing properly.

The excruciatingly complicated answer. . .

The speed at which you grow is controlled by a hormone produced in your brain. So what exactly is a hormone? I'm afraid you've got to know this before you can begin to understand the excruciatingly complicated answer. . .

Horrible hormones fact file

Name of body part: Hormones

Where found: Made by glands in different parts of the body

Useful things they do: Cause changes in the body. For example, some hormones give teenagers a grown-up appearance.

Grisly details: Hormones cause horrible problems (see below).

Amazing features: Cortisol (cor-tis-sol), made by the adrenal glands, is a chemical alarm clock that wakes you up!

Where to find your glands. . .

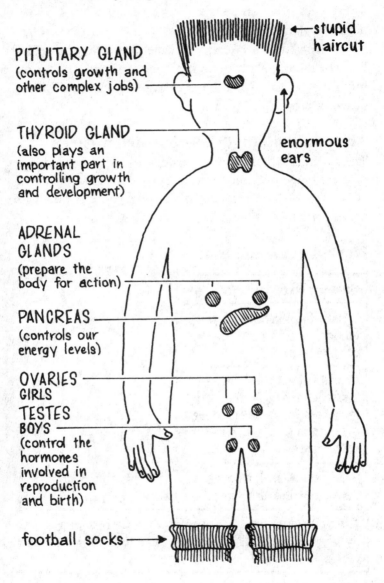

← stupid haircut

PITUITARY GLAND
(controls growth and
other complex jobs)

THYROID GLAND
(also plays an
important part in
controlling growth
and development)

enormous
ears

**ADRENAL
GLANDS**
(prepare the
body for action)

PANCREAS
(controls our
energy levels)

OVARIES
GIRLS

TESTES
BOYS
(control the
hormones
involved in
reproduction
and birth)

football socks →

Horrible hormone problems

Here lies the answer to the question, "Why do people grow?" The pituitary also makes the hormone that tells your body to grow! Growth hormone burrows through a cell and into the nucleus to meet – the genes. The hormone tells the genes to order the cells to grow and divide so your body can grow. So what on earth are genes? (Told you this was complicated!)

Bet you never knew!
Genes are found on 46 stringy objects called chromosomes. They contain a chemical code that tells the body what it should look like. This code stores an awesome amount of information. If you wrote out the code from just one cell in letters the size of the words in this book it would be 10,000 km (6210 miles) long.

CHROMOSOMES

Growing places

Your relatives might think you've grown quite a bit in the last year but that's nothing to the amount of growing you did before you were born. You probably can't remember that far back – so here's what happened.

Most animals mate to make new offspring. (The only creatures that don't are tiny jelly-like things that you can only see through a microscope. They split in two – which

153

sounds really painful.) But we humans also mate to make children. Well, just imagine your poor parents having to split in two to make your little brother!

The aim of mating is to allow the male and female parents to mix their genes up. That's why children end up looking a bit like both their parents.

THAT'S OUR BOY!

The genes are carried in special cells called sperm and eggs. The male makes sperm cells in his testes and the female releases an egg cell from her ovaries. (In humans the egg cell is far smaller than a hen's egg – in fact you need a microscope to see it at all!) The male releases 400,000,000 tiny tadpole-like sperm at a time but only one of these manages to dive into the egg to make a baby.

Baby-builders

The egg now divides into two cells, and these divide to make 4, 8, 16, 32, 64, 128, 256, 512, 1,024, 2,048, 4,096, 8,192, 16,384, 32,768, 65,536 cells and so on. (You continue this list if you really want!)

So from two original cells come all the cells in the body – your muscles, bones, teeth, brain, liver, eyeballs, sweat-glands and everything else. This process of division and sorting goes on until the tiny ball of cells turns into a baby. A tiny, incredible, brand-new human being.

Incredible infancy

Now you might think that babies are pretty useless and definitely disgusting. After all, they do nothing much except sleep, dribble, throw up and other unmentionable things. But babies are incredible (just ask their mums and dads!) and babyhood is an incredible time for the body. Which of the following are too amazing to be true?

1 In the 238 days before birth a baby's weight increases 5 million times. (Lucky you don't put on weight so quickly nowadays!) TRUE / FALSE

2 During this time a baby floats around happily in a salty pool inside it's mum's womb. It turns somersaults and even scratches itself with its fingernails. TRUE / FALSE

UMBILICAL CORD

BABY AFTER 36 WEEKS

CAN'T WAIT TO STRETCH MY LEGS!

3 The baby is fed from the mother through a tube called the umbilical cord that passes through its belly button. TRUE / FALSE

4 Babies go through a stage before they are born when they are covered in tiny hairs. TRUE / FALSE

5 Babies have a natural sense of rhythm. They kick their little hands and feet in time to music even before they are born. TRUE / FALSE

6 When they are born babies can't see in colour, only in

black and white. TRUE / FALSE

7 Babies can taste food better than grown-ups because they have about 9,000 more taste-buds. TRUE / FALSE

8 Babies can remember faces. TRUE / FALSE

9 A baby can tell when someone is talking in a foreign language. TRUE / FALSE

10 Babies sleep more but dream less than adults. TRUE / FALSE

In the first year after they are born, babies get 6.3 kg (1 stone) heavier. Within two years they can walk and talk. At five they're old enough to go to school. And after that it's downhill all the way.

Appalling old age

Age does funny things to people. The older a grown-up gets the less willing they are to admit how old they are. You might think that your teacher is about 98. But if you dare to ask him he might well say, "I'm in the prime of life." (Teachers are ALIVE?!) Well anyway, here are a few sure signs of ageing to look out for in your teachers.

Losing hair
Lazy pupils*
Hairy ears
Deafness
Grey hair
Hairy nostrils
Dry and wrinkly skin
Shuffling walk
Jutting chin
Blotchy skin
Trembling hands
Put on weight

* That's slow-moving eyes – not the pupils he teaches.

AMAZING old age

BUT don't assume that your poor old teacher is a clapped-out old has-been. Remember . . . older people (and that includes your more mature teachers) have a vast store of wisdom and learning. Many famous people have made their greatest contribution to world history in their later years.

• Genghis Khan (1162-1227) the Mongolian soldier was

conquering most of the known world when he was in his sixties.

• William Gladstone (1809-1898) was Prime Minister of Britain when he was in his eighties.

• In a single year, English novelist Barbara Cartland wrote 26 books. She was 82 at the time.

• Shirali Mislimov of Georgia was born in 1806 and his youngest child was born in 1937 when he was 131. And Old Shirali was still going strong in 1973 at the age of 168!

The horrible truth

Nobody's perfect. And no body is perfect either. Every body ages, aches and suffers from disgusting diseases. Sometimes its bones get broken, too. A few scientists thought they could make something better than a human body. A new improved home-made body or a machine that could replace the body.

But was it worth the effort? For all its faults, the body is the most fantastic, the most incredible machine in the entire universe. And it's all yours! Your body can do things that no machine could ever do. It can grow, and when it works harder its muscles grow too. It can walk thousands of kilometres and not wear out. The soles of its feet even renew themselves and thicken to make walking easier.

Your body can do 101 different things, and the most amazing thing of all is that you can do them ALL AT ONCE!

• You can ride a bicycle and digest your dinner.

• Kick a football and imagine you're playing in the Cup Final.

• You can listen to music and do your homework and still guzzle a packet of crisps!

The body suffers from disgusting diseases, it's true. But then it gets better. It actually heals and repairs itself. All you have to do is to give it proper food and exercise. Treat your body well and it'll last a lifetime.

Of course, if you went into Dr Frankenstein's lab and saw all the body bits, the bones and bottles of blood you might say, "Yuck! How horrible!"

But you've also got to admit that the body is more than just horrible. It's horribly amazing too! And that's horrible science for you!

CHEMICAL CHAOS

Introduction

Chemistry can be summed up in a single word – "UGH!". It's that part of science to do with chemicals and test tubes. "Ugh!" is the best word for it! It's the most *horrible* part of Horrible Science.

And why is it so horrible? Well – if you find science confusing you'll find chemistry as clear as mud. It can cause chaos in your brain.

For starters, there are those chaotic-sounding chemical names. Like poly methyl metha crylate* (say polly me-thile-me-tha-cry-late). *That's the acrylic in your jumper, if you didn't already know.

THAT'S AN ATTRACTIVE POLYACRYLONITRITE JUMPER YOU'RE WEARING!*

*TRANSLATION – I LIKE YOUR ACRYLIC JUMPER

These long words are mainly Latin or Greek. Fine for ancient Romans – but horribly confusing for the rest of us. Sometimes chemistry turns totally chaotic. That's when chemists talk their own chaotic code language.

THIS H_2O HASN'T YET REACHED 100°

I REQUIRE SOME $C_{12}H_{22}O_{11}$

THIS LACTIC ACID SMELLS UNPLEASANT

Translation:

1 The water hasn't boiled.

2 Pass the sugar.

3 Lactic acid = sour milk: the milk's gorn orf!

Even a chemist's brain seems pretty chaotic. How else would they come to investigate soggy cornflakes? (Chemists have reported that a cornflake with more than 18% milk content is just too soggy to study.)

But funnily enough that's what this book is about. Not the bits you learn in school – but the funny bits and the fascinating bits, the bits you really want to find out about ... nasty bubbling green mixtures, vile and sometimes poisonous potions, test tubes, horrible smells, bangs, blasts and dodgy discoveries.

But *Chemical Chaos* might just help you see through the confusion that is chemistry, then you might just end up causing chaos in your chemistry teacher's day, by getting your own experiments to work...

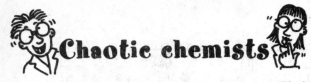

Chaotic chemists

Chemists are curiously chaotic. Their knowledge of chemicals used to be chaotically confused and their messed-up experiments caused chaos too. The first chemists were called alchemists and they were pretty chaotic. And strange.

Imagine it's a particularly boring chemistry lesson, and you are feeling ver-r-ry sleepy. The next thing you know you are in a mysterious room... You see an old man reading a book. He is surrounded by oddly-shaped flasks, the stumps of candles and dirty beakers. On a nearby table there are bottles of ink, tatty goose feather pens, oily rags and old musty books – full of ancient dust and secrets. In the chaotic shadows stand row upon row of bottles filled with weird potions. On the floor lie the rat-nibbled remains of several meals. The old man laughs to himself. Then in a thin crackly voice he reads a magical spell...

EYE OF NEWT,
WING OF BAT,
FOOTBALL BOOT,
TAIL OF CAT!

Confused? Don't worry this is **NOT** your chemistry teacher! You've just slipped back 500 years to meet your local chemist. Except 500 years ago chemists weren't called chemists – they were called alchemists.

A note to the reader

Dear reader, as far as this book is concerned a chemist is NOT a shop where you buy pills. A chemist is someone who studies chemicals. O.K.?

Appalling alchemists

Alchemy started in Egypt in Roman times and in ancient China. It's a mixture of chemical knowledge, magic and philosophy about how materials are formed. On a more practical level, alchemists tried to turn cheap metals into gold. Here's one of their more unusual recipes.

YE OLD ALCHEMIST'S RECIPE FOR MAKING GOLD.

1. Take some alum (that's a compound of aluminium, sulphur, potassium and oxygen).

2. Add some coal dust, pyrites (iron ore) and a few drops of mercury (the runny metal found in thermometers).

3. Mix well.

4. Stir in an ounce of cinnamon (spicy-tasting tree-bark) and half a dozen egg yolks. Keep stirring until the mixture is gooey.

5. Then add a generous dollop of fresh horse dung. Keep stirring.

6. Finally, add some sal ammoniac. (This is a poisonous mixture of ammonia and chlorine found in volcanoes.)

7. Bake well in a hot oven for six hours. The result should be pure gold. If you're lucky.

A note to the reader:

Dear reader, don't bother trying this for yourself. It doesn't work— honest!

Although some people poked fun at its more curious notions – alchemy was fashionable. Even kings wanted to try it. It has been suggested that the British King Charles II was poisoned by the mercury he used for alchemy experiments. His scientist pal Sir Isaac Newton used this substance for experiments and went mad for two years.

> *Bet you never knew!*
> One famous alchemist was the Arab writer Geber (or Jeber). Now old Geb had lots of ideas but he was a lousy writer. In fact, his boring books of experiments gave rise to the word "gibberish". Sadly, Geber wasn't the last scientist to come out with a load of old gibberish.

Here's another alchemist's trick you shouldn't try.

To warm a liquid

Surround a jar of the liquid with horse manure. Germs in the dung cause chemical reactions which produce heat. This really works – but if you do want to keep your tea warm try a thermos flask – it's less smelly!

Get-rich Rutherford?

Despite many failures the alchemists kept going. They believed a substance called the "philosopher's stone" would turn cheap metals into gold. No one knew what the philosopher's stone was exactly or where to find it. But alchemists were convinced that the person who found the stone would live for ever. Of course, no one ever discovered the real answer. Until quite recently...

In 1911 New Zealander Ernest Rutherford (1871-1937) found out how to change metals into gold. This involved the metals' atoms, which are the minuscule objects that make up all substances. To make the gold, you zap bits off the atoms with a high-energy ray. By changing the atoms you can change the metal they form.

But Rutherford had bad news for alchemists:

1 Atoms are so tiny they're easy to miss with your zapping ray.

2 The easiest metal to turn into gold is platinum. But that's even more expensive than gold!

I WONDER IF YOU CAN TURN GOLD BACK INTO PLATINUM?

3 So if you want gold it really is cheaper to buy some from your local jeweller!

Chaotic chemists of the past

By 1700 scientists were becoming curious about chemicals for reasons other than alchemy. They dropped the "al" bit as well, and called themselves "chemists" instead. "Al" only means "the" in Arabic anyway. But many people thought chemistry was a strange idea. One scientist, Justus von Liebig (1803-1873) was told off at school for not doing homework. His teacher asked him what job he wanted to do and Justus said he wanted to be a chemist whereupon...

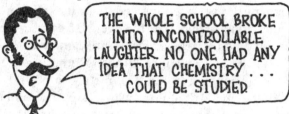

THE WHOLE SCHOOL BROKE INTO UNCONTROLLABLE LAUGHTER. NO ONE HAD ANY IDEA THAT CHEMISTRY... COULD BE STUDIED

One man played a vital role in begining to change their minds. His name was Antoine Lavoisier (1743-1794). Some people even called him the "Father of Modern Chemistry". But in 1789 revolution swept France and Lavoisier found himself in a seriously chaotic situation.

An enemy of the people?

It was a time of terror but no one dared use the word. No one was safe from arrest. In the Square of the Revolution there were daily executions for the old women to watch as they sat knitting in the spring sunshine.

MERCY!

WHY DO THEY ALWAYS SAY "THANKYOU"?

"Pass me ze papers," said the Public Prosecutor to his newly-appointed clerk. "Yes, the ones about Citizen Lavoisier."

The young man hurriedly searched his desk. It was unwise to waste the Prosecutor's time. The Prosecutor, Antoine Fouquier-Tinville, was always in a hurry.

"*Merci* – thank you," said the Prosecutor, and he hastily examined the paper. "Aha, Antoine Lavoisier – the collector of taxes..."

"He's a great scientist too..." ventured the clerk.

"WHO dares say so!" screamed the Prosecutor.

The clerk dropped his quill pen and papers in a shower of ink. "I mean, I didn't mean that!" he stammered. "I meant Lavoisier is a great traitor! Oh, silly me!"

"Well," said the Prosecutor, "let's see what the file says." He began reading the document in the harsh voice he used to terrify prisoners in court:

"Antoine Lavoisier. Born 1743 and brought up by his aunt, father and grandmother ... Hmm – he was a swot at school. Spent one year in which his only lessons were science and maths. Pah! Two more years learning nothing but philosophy. Pah! Pah! Wrote his first scientific paper at the age of ten – what a little creep! Later found gypsum has water in it and mineral water has tiny bits of salt. Very useful ... I *don't* think. Ha, ha!"

"I ... I know," said the clerk from the floor in a small

voice, "that Lavoisier *is* a traitor ... but ... he did find that water contains hydrogen and oxygen chemicals. Then he discovered gases in the air. Then he found you can't destroy chemicals – only change them around and then..."

"Stop, you fool!" spat the Prosecutor. "Do you think I need ze chemistry lesson?! Ah – here's the juicy bit. In 1768 Citizen Lavoisier became a *tax* collector. One of his friends said, 'The dinners he will give us will be so much the better!' All the tax collectors are the enemies of the people. Thanks to the revolution they're in prison now!"

The Prosecutor smiled unpleasantly. "Let's see if they enjoy their fine dinners without their heads on!" He drew his finger across his throat and made a choking sound.

"Excuse me – I've got some papers to file!" said the clerk as he fled the room in panic. He just missed a thin man in a green coat. The visitor was plainly dressed apart from his white powdered hair. He certainly didn't look like the most powerful man in France. But that's who he was.

"Citizen Robespierre," said the Public Prosecutor with a false smile. "This is indeed a pleasure and an honour. The papers await your signature."

"More enemies of the people?" enquired Robespierre. He seated himself without being asked and read the document. "Lavoisier. Yes, I remember him. He supported the revolution at first. Helped with the new metric weights too. He did good work for France running gunpowder factories before the revolution. He would be a great loss."

The Prosecutor frowned. He was unsure if Robespierre was testing his loyalty and replied nervously, "Our revolutionary hero, Citizen Marat, called

Lavoisier a traitor in his newspaper articles."

"Yes, I know," said Robespierre. "But Marat was a failed scientist and Lavoisier was rude enough to say so. That's why Marat hated him so much."

"So. You mean us to spare Citizen Lavoisier?"

Robespierre merely smiled coldly and gazed out of the window. The pen was poised like a dagger in his hand.

Antoine Lavoisier's trial began on 8 May, 1794. The scientist looked pale and tired after six months in prison. He pleaded for more time to finish a vital chemistry experiment. Would Robespierre take pity on him? What do *you* think the verdict was?

a) GUILTY. The Judge said, "The Republic has no need for scientists." and Lavoisier was beheaded that afternoon.

b) NOT GUILTY. The Judge said, "The Republic should spare the life of such a great scientist."

c) GUILTY. The Judge said, "But we'll give you a month to finish off your experiment."

Answer: a) One of Lavoisier's friends said, "It took them only an instant to cut off that head, and another hundred years may not produce another like it." Two months later Robespierre lost power and was put to death. Fouquier-Tinville was executed the following year. And Lavoisier's work lives on...

173

Chaotic contemporary chemists

Nowadays, there are thousands of chemists. In the USA alone there are over 140,000 chemists trying to discover new chemicals! Some are looking for ultra-light metals or new kinds of plastics. Others are looking for new food ingredients or medical drugs. Here's where they work.

A Chemistry Lab

At first sight all these bits and pieces look a bit funny. But they all have their uses.

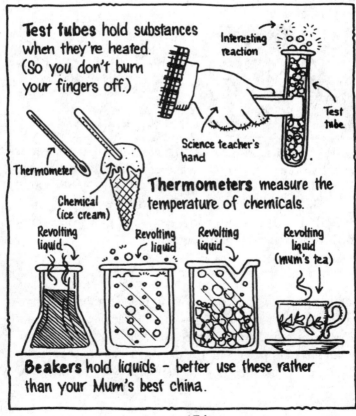

Test tubes hold substances when they're heated. (So you don't burn your fingers off.)

Interesting reaction

Test tube

Science teacher's hand

Thermometer

Chemical (ice cream)

Thermometers measure the temperature of chemicals.

Revolting liquid

Revolting liquid

Revolting liquid

Revolting liquid (mum's tea)

Beakers hold liquids – better use these rather than your Mum's best china.

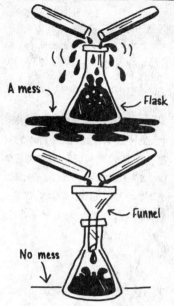

Flasks are for mixing chemicals in. They're usually conical in shape – that means they're shaped like a cone – and have flat bottoms.

A mess

Flask

Funnels for pouring mixtures into flasks without slopping them all over the floor (see above).

Funnel

No mess

Filter paper

Fold here

Filter paper – a paper sieve for separating solid chemicals from a liquid. The runny bit passes through paper and solid lumps get caught. It's a bit like making filter coffee really.

Fits in funnel

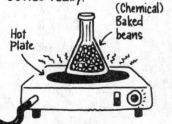

Hot Plate

(Chemical) Baked beans

Hot plates – a bit like cooker tops. Ideal for heating and cooking dinner too.

175

Droppers for measuring little drips of chemicals.

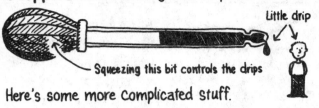

Little drip

Squeezing this bit controls the drips

Here's some more complicated stuff.

A gas chromatograph
Inside this mysterious machine are chemicals that absorb and so separate out the chemicals in your favourite stinky gas. That way you'll know what goes to make up that lovely pong.

A spectroscope allows you to spot a chemical from a pattern of lights and colours given off when it is heated up.
It's a bit like watching your very own colour TV.

Bet you never knew!
These days robots do many of the boring jobs in a lab such as testing samples. Pity they can't get robots to do science homework, too!

Dare you discover ... your own secret substance?

If being a chemist sounds like fun here's your chance to make a laughably easy discovery.

You will need:

2 teaspoonfuls of cream of tartar (available from supermarkets)

1 cup of salt

2 cups of plain flour

2 cups of water

2 tablespoonfuls of cooking oil

All you do is:

1 Mix the flour and salt in a large saucepan.

2 Add the water and mix well.

3 Add the cream of tartar and the cooking oil and mix well.

4 Ask an adult to help you heat the saucepan on a low heat and stir it until the mixture thickens. Leave to cool.

Like any other inventor you'll need to find a use for your new discovery. That's up to you – here's a few daft ideas.

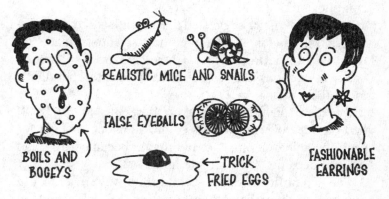

REALISTIC MICE AND SNAILS

FALSE EYEBALLS

BOILS AND BOGEYS

←TRICK FRIED EGGS

FASHIONABLE EARRINGS

Finally, you'll need to dream up a name for your new substance ... any suggestions?

Chaotic chemical expressions

Were chemists just having a laugh when they thought up names like polyvinylidenechloride? What do you think they were talking about?

Answer: That's clingfilm to you.

What's in a name?

So, how do scientists decide on a name for all these new substances? And do they have to be so long and complicated?

1 In 1787 Lavoisier suggested that scientists should agree names for chemicals. Before then scientists made up their own mysterious names. Chemical names still sound pretty mysterious but you can be sure your teacher didn't make them up.

2 Swedish scientist Jöns Jakob Berzelius (1779-1848) had the idea of using letters of the alphabet to stand for each chemical atom. So hydrogen became "H" and oxygen became "O" – simple innit?

3 The scientific Swede's second brainwave was to use numbers to show the numbers of atoms in each chemical. So H_2 means "two hydrogen atoms". Brilliant – eh?

4 When you get two or more atoms joined together it's

called a molecule. $2H_2$ means two lots of two hydrogen atoms and H_2O is a molecule of the two hydrogen atoms and an oxygen atom joined together.

5 In fact H_2O is just the chemists' code for plain boring old water.

But anyone can be a chemist. In fact, you may be one without even realizing it. And if that sounds incredible – consider this: you use chemistry every time you cook or wash up. Shocking, isn't it?

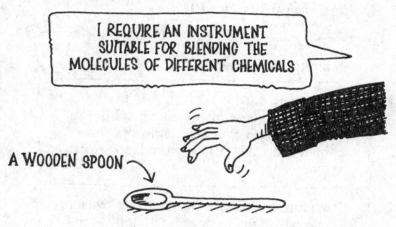

I REQUIRE AN INSTRUMENT SUITABLE FOR BLENDING THE MOLECULES OF DIFFERENT CHEMICALS

A WOODEN SPOON

Chaotic kitchen chemistry

How can cookery possibly be chemical? Actually, it would be impossible to cook without chemistry. It's what cooking's all about – from the suspect substances that call themselves school dinners, to the revolting reaction that makes your dad's homemade rice pudding stick to its dish.

Cooking chemicals fact file

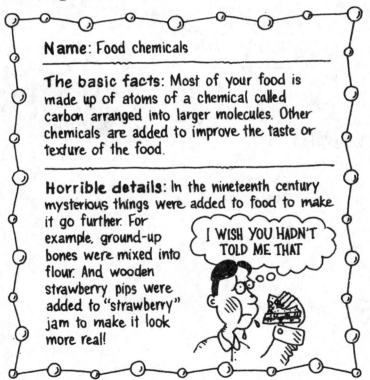

Name: Food chemicals

The basic facts: Most of your food is made up of atoms of a chemical called carbon arranged into larger molecules. Other chemicals are added to improve the taste or texture of the food.

Horrible details: In the nineteenth century mysterious things were added to food to make it go further. For example, ground-up bones were mixed into flour. And wooden strawberry pips were added to "strawberry" jam to make it look more real!

I WISH YOU HADN'T TOLD ME THAT

Kitchen chemistry lab

It's a strange thought, but your kitchen is a bit like a chemistry lab.

Some machines in your kitchen are mysteriously similar to instruments used by scientists.

Pressure cooker

This works by allowing water to boil at a higher temperature than usual, so it cooks things faster. But it's similar to a machine called an autoclave that kills germs on scientific instruments.

Thermos flask

This is handy for keeping your soup hot or a drink cold on a summer's day. But the flask was originally invented by a chemist. In 1892 Sir James Dewar invented the double-walled container to keep his chemicals cold.

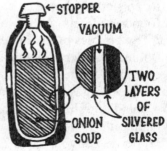

Cooker

This is simply a machine for heating food chemicals to produce the chemical reactions that we call cooking.

Here are some fascinating food facts to impress your friends during school lunchbreak. (You'll impress them even more if you can work out what you're eating.)

Six mixed-up food facts

1 The burning sensation you get if you eat chilli peppers is due to a chemical called capsaicin (cap-say-kin). According to experts the best remedy for a fiery mouth is a generous helping of ice-cream! That's tragic!

2 The smell of raspberries found in most yoghurts is due to an added chemical called ionone. It was originally found in violets. Aah!

3 The bubbles in a cooked cake mixture are made by gas! Baking powder contains an acid and a chemical rich in carbon. When they're heated, a chemical reaction produces a gas called carbon dioxide.

4 Salad dressing is an emulsion. No, that's not a type of paint. It's a mixture of two chemicals that don't mix properly. Leave a salad dressing for a few hours and it will turn into a layer of oil above a layer of vinegar.

5 Vinegar is made from wine that has gone disgustingly sour. This chemical reaction is caused by the waste products produced by germs. Yuck!

6 Toast is bread in which the carbon has been partly burnt. The smoke that sometimes pours from the toaster is made from tiny bits of carbon.

FRESH CARBON – MY FAVOURITE!

Teacher's Tea-Break Teasers

If you are very brave (or foolhardy) knock on the door of the staffroom and try this question on your teacher.

STAFF ROOM

SOME PEOPLE ADD TEA TO MILK AND SOME ADD MILK TO TEA IN THE CUP. IS THERE ANY DIFFERENCE IN THE TASTE AND IF SO WHY?

Answer: It does make a difference. Milk contains a chemical called casein (case-in). When tea mixes with milk its chemicals break down the casein into smaller molecules. If you add the milk to the tea it means that more casein gets broken down. This makes the tea taste of boiled milk. That's why chemists in the know add tea to milk and not the other way around!

Amazing changes

Like tea-making, cooking is about heating chemicals until they change in some way. For example, chips cook at 190°C (374°F) and meringues need several hours at 70°C (158°F). But what causes these dramatic changes?

Try these terrible trick questions on your unsuspecting cookery teacher!

1 When you are trying to boil milk why does it suddenly go "whoosh" and try to leap out of the pan?

2 The boiling point of cooking oil is hotter than the temperature needed to melt a frying pan. So how can you fry food?

Answers: 1 The milk contains fat globules that form a layer on the top of the liquid as it heats. At about 100°C the milk under the fat layer is a frenzy of boiling bubbles. Suddenly the fat layer splits allowing the milk to whoosh! **2** The food contains water that boils at its usual temperature. This boiling water cooks the food and the oil doesn't boil at all.

Foul fertilizers

Even your vegetables are not free from the mysterious activities of the chemical industry. There's a whole array of herbicides, insecticides, fungicides and pesticides sprayed on the growing plants to deter ugly bugs and weeds. Then there are *fertilizers* to make crops grow.

HOW DARE YOU! I WOULDN'T TOUCH THE STUFF!

Phosphorous may be poisonous for humans but it's good for making fertilizer chemicals called phosphates. One traditional type of naturally phosphate-rich fertilizer is guano. It's found several metres deep on islands off the coast of Peru. And the origin of this special substance ... do you really want to know? Old seabird droppings full of digested fish bones. Oh yes – bones are rich in phosphates and ground-up bones are ideal for growing plants.

Nowadays fertilizers are made by mixing sulphuric acid with phosphates found in rocks. But the chemists have not just stuck to fertilizers. Some *foods* were practically invented in a test-tube.

A slippery story – margarine

French Emperor Napoleon III organized a competition to invent a cheap butter-substitute for poor people.

Scientist Hippolyte Mége-Mouriez reckoned that anything a cow could do HE could do better.

In 1869 he came up with his magic marg ingredients:

INGREDIENTS
beef fat
skimmed milk
ice
pig's stomach
juices

UGH!

Method

1 Simply heat the beef fat to the body temperature of a cow.

2 Gradually pour in pigs' stomach juices.

3 Stir in the water and milk.

4 Now churn the ingredients together in a handy barrel.

5 Add ice to cool the mixture.

6 Squelch it all together.

Mouriez hoped to get rich and he opened a factory to make margarine. Unfortunately, war broke out between France and Prussia and his factory had to close down.

GONE TO WAR, BACK IN TWO YEARS.

BLUB

Two years later the idea was bought by a couple of Dutch merchants. Soon they were churning out margarine and profits.

In 1910 a shortage of animal fat led to the use of vegetable oils or smelly fish oil.

Looking at the ingredients

Most foods you can buy in a supermarket have the ingredients on the side. Some sound a bit weird. Margarine, for example usually contains...
• hydrogenated oils
• emulsifier
• anti-oxidants
• vitamins
• water

YUK! I **CAN** BELIEVE IT'S NOT BUTTER!

Emulsifiers are chemicals with two ends. One likes oils and one likes water. So this marvellous molecule cleverly joins the water and the oil molecules together.

Anti-oxidants stop the margarine going off, or rancid. Sage and rosemary plants include natural anti-oxidants often used by food manufacturers.

Hydrogenation means adding a type of chemical called hydrogen to the margarine. This makes the marg harder and more like butter.

Vitamins are a group of different chemicals you can get from different foods. Vitamins keep your body healthy. Margarine doesn't contain some vitamins so they are added to make it healthier to eat.

Chaotic chemical cookery

Besides margarine, lots of chemists have made food from chemicals you definitely wouldn't want to eat.

1 Alexander Butlerov (1828-1886) found that formaldehyde (for-mal-de-hide) can be treated to make a type of sugar called glucose. Formaldehyde is a horrible smelly chemical used to preserve bits of dead body.

2 During the Second World War German chemists discovered how to make fat from oil – not cooking oils but the sort of oil you put in a car! Mmm, tasty!

Dare you discover ... some chemical cookery?

Try creating a little bit of chemical chaos in your kitchen with these experimental recipes.

1 *Yucky yeast*

Yeast is no mere chemical. It's ALIVE! Yes – yeast is a tiny fungus like the mould that grows on stale bread. Ugh! Yeast is harmless but its horrible relatives can cause

skin infections and some diseases of the lungs and guts.
You will need:
some dried yeast (you can get packets from supermarkets)
2 teaspoons and a tablespoon
a small bowl or mug
sugar
warm water

All you do is:
1 Mix 2 teaspoonfuls of yeast with 2 tablespoonfuls of warm water in the bowl.
2 Stir in a tablespoonful of sugar until it dissolves.
3 Stir in a teaspoon of dried yeast.
4 Leave the bowl in a warm place for an hour and check what's happened.

a) The mixture has turned bright red.
b) The liquid froths up and has a funny smell.
c) Small crystals have formed in the mixture and it stinks.

Answer: b) The yeast eats up the sugar and produces alcohol and carbon dioxide – that's the froth. This is also what happens when people make wine from grape juice.

2 *Terrific toffee*
Sugar is a complicated compound (mixture) of chemicals including carbon, hydrogen and oxygen atoms. Many sweets

189

are simply sugar that's been heated to a particular temperature. For example, fudge is made at 116°C (241°F), caramel at 120°C (248°F) and the hottest of all ... toffee. Here's how to make it.

You will need:
an adult to help you
25 g (1 ounce) butter
100 g (4 ounces) castor sugar
7.5 ml water
a sugar thermometer
a tablespoon and saucepan
a bowl of ice-cold water
some chopped apple with skin attached
enough cocktail sticks for every bit of apple

All you do is:
1 Stick a cocktail stick in each of the chopped apple pieces.
2 Mix the sugar, water and butter in the saucepan.
3 Heat the mixture to 160°C (320°F). Stir it gently. Notice how the sugar turns into a brown, melted, gungey mass on the way.
4 Dip some apple in the mixture. Be careful – it's very hot! Then dip the apple into the cold water for about 20 seconds to cool it down.
5 Eat it!

And after that there's nothing else for it – you've got to wash up. It's a mystery where half the washing-up comes from. Never mind, even the really great scientists had to do this. And luckily, there's lots of chemical cleaners to help you!

Squeaky cleaners

There's bound to be a few squeaks of protest when it comes to washing greasy dishes or getting soggy in a boring old bath. But it's got to be done, so where would we be without cleaning chemicals? Somewhere disgustingly dirty – that's where!

Soapy secrets fact file

Name: Soap

The basic facts: Soap is a salt made from acids and alkalis taken from fats. Soap is the layer you skim off the top of the mixture.

Horrible details: The Romans washed in soap to treat elephantiasis, a truly disgusting disease in which tiny worms get under the skin. The soap was useless as a cure.

IT'S NOT WORKING

A soap opera

1 The first soap was mixed-up fat and wood ash. It was probably invented when someone's cookery went chaotically wrong.

2 Soap was used in France about 2,000 years ago by an ancient people called the Gauls. They claimed that soap made from goat fat kept their hair nice and shiny.

3 Eighteenth-century soap was made by mixing boiling fat and soda. The alkaline soda makes the fat turn into soap. But too much of the alkali dissolves the skin! Nasty.

4 Luckily, before 1853 soap was so heavily taxed that many people couldn't afford to use it.

5 In 1900 people washed clothes using soap. (Washing powder hadn't been invented then.) The soap turned clothes yellow, so clothes were then dyed blue. This had the effect of making them appear white again.

6 Between 1911 and 1980 British people doubled the amount of soap they used each year. Did that mean twice as many baths?

Super soap

Soap is great for washing things because of the shape of the soap molecule. It has a long tail that sticks to dirt and a head end that's attracted to water molecules by an electrical force. The result? The soap molecule yanks the dirt into the water. Then you can wash the dirt away.

Dare you discover ... a slippery soap experiment?

You will need:
two mirrors
a bathroom
soap

All you have to do is:
1 Rub one mirror with a thin layer of soap.
2 Run the hot tap. Only one of the mirrors steams up.
Which one is it ... and why?

THIS COULD BE TRICKY...

a) The soapy mirror steams up because soap attracts the water in the steam.
b) The soapy mirror doesn't steam up or get wet because the soap stops the water getting to the glass.
c) The soapy mirror gets wet but doesn't steam up. The soap stops the water in the steam forming droplets on the glass.

Answer: c)

Detergent – what's in it for you?

The first detergents were developed by the Germans during the First World War. They were originally developed from coal tar. During that war the Germans had a smelly problem owing to a shortage of soap, so they used detergents instead. But these were useless – you had to rub really hard before you got any froth. But as luck would have it – the new detergent worked wonders on their woollies!

DETERGENT
USELESS ON SKIN BUT GREAT ON JUMPERS!

Eating up the dirt

It's amazing what they fit in a box of washing powder. For example, "biological" washing powders include enzymes. These are chemicals often found in living creatures that cause reactions between other chemicals. Washing powder enzymes help to gobble up nasty stains such as blood and egg and disgusting little bits of food. The enzyme molecules stay the same.

WASHING POWDER ENZYME

BLOOD AND EGG – SCRUMMY!

Action-packed powders

Here are some other things you'll find in a packet of

washing powder.

Builders – these are nothing to do with construction workers! These are chemicals that remove dirt and stop it sticking to anything else in the wash.

Anti-rusting chemicals stop rust from eating away your washing machine's vital innards.

Conditioners stop the grains of powder sticking together and help them to dissolve in the washing water.

Optical brighteners are chemicals that soak up ordinary light and reflect back bluish light. This makes your undies appear whiter than white. Just a clever chemical trick, really.

Dirt-bouncers are other chemicals that give dirt a tiny electrical force, making it bounce off your washing.

HORRIBLE SCIENCE HEALTH WARNING

...AND DON'T MISTAKE IT FOR SHAMPOO LIKE I DID

Some cleaning materials such as caustic soda and oven cleaner contain horribly unpleasant chemicals. They dissolve germs – but make sure you stay clear of them. They're very good at dissolving fingers too!

Chemical chaos in the bathroom

Your bathroom is brimming with amazing chemicals.

1 The water in your taps contains salts. It also contains calcium and magnesium salts dissolved from rocks in the ground.

2 If there is a lot of calcium and magnesium in the water it is called "hard water" and forms a revolting scum when you try to lather soap.

3 Boiling hard water changes the dissolved chemicals into chemicals that *won't* dissolve. That's how you get a disgusting deposit of limescale. Limescale is actually calcium carbonate – the same chemical found in chalk. You may find it lurking inside electric kettles too.

4 The first toilet cleaners were made from explosives! They were invented in 1919 when heating engineer

Harry Pickup was removing explosive waste from an ammunition factory. He dropped some in a toilet and found that the substance – nitrecake – is brilliant at cleaning. Flushed with his success, Harry opened a factory and soon became rich.

5 Talcum powder comes from volcanoes. Yes – it's true. Talc is a chemical called magnesium silicate. It's found in rocks that have been chemically changed by underground heat.

6 Toothpastes sometimes contain pumice which is another rock produced by volcanoes. (You may find pumice lurking in your bathroom anyway. It's used for scrubbing away at hard skin.)

7 Toothpaste is designed to brush away germs and stray bits of food. The first toothpastes were made from gritty substances such as chalk and jeweller's polish. They certainly wore away those nasty little stains – but they wore away people's teeth too!

Dare you discover ... how to make your own toothpaste?

You will need:

salt
sugar
a bowl and spoon

All you do is:

1 Mix the salt and sugar with a little water to make a paste.

2 Try it on your teeth.

Note: These ingredients really were used in the nineteenth century to make toothpaste. But don't *you* try them more than once. The sugar's not good for your teeth. In fact, you'd better use some proper toothpaste to remove your home-made version! Some experiments should never be repeated.

Toothpaste is just one of a huge array of strange but useful substances dreamt up by chemists. Funnily enough, chemical chaos often led to some amazing accidental discoveries.

O.K. – SO IT DIDN'T CURE MY BALDNESS, BUT MY HEARING IS A THOUSAND TIMES BETTER

Dodgy discoveries

EUREKA!

A chaotic combination of muddles, mishaps and mix-ups – that's how many a vital substance has been discovered. Scientists have to keep their minds open to anything that might happen during an experiment, but sometimes they might set out to answer one question, and end up solving another.

Chaotic chemists' comments...

Here's how some chaotic chemists describe their discoveries. Test them out on your science teacher.

"No great discovery is ever made without a bold guess."

Sir Isaac Newton (1642-1727) discoverer of gravity and big fan of alchemy.

"Failure is the mother of success."

Hideki Yukawa (1907-1981) who discovered what some of the tiny bits of atoms are made of.

"The most important of my discoveries have been suggested by my failures."

Sir Humphry Davy (1778-1829) discoverer of many new chemicals.

Many surprising substances all owe their discovery to happy accidents.

Eight dodgy discoveries

1 One inventor was supposedly inspired by his wife's cookery. She kept getting food stuck to the bottom of the saucepan – so he developed a teflon coated non-stick pan to solve this sticky problem.

2 *Tracing paper* was invented by mistake in the 1930s because a worker at a paper factory put too much starch in a vat of wood pulp. The result was strong but see-though paper

3 *Paper tissues* were designed as a new kind of make-up remover. In 1924, they were sold as disposable handkerchiefs after people wrote in saying the pads were ideal for blowing their noses.

4 *Vulcanized rubber* Early rubber boots melted in hot weather. But in 1844 Charles Goodyear spilt some boiling rubber and sulphur. He found that the resulting sticky mess didn't melt so easily.

5 *Silly Putty* the bouncy modelling clay, was discovered in 1943 when scientists attempted to make artificial rubber from silicon. The substance was no good for tyres

but the chemists had a lot of fun playing with it. A sharp-eyed salesman spotted the opportunity to develop a new toy and sold 750,000 Silly Putty balls in three days.

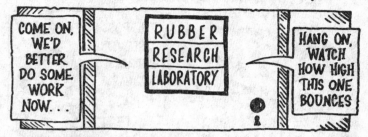

6 *Lubricating oil* was first sold in 1690 as a cure for the painful joint disease, rheumatism. The chaotic idea was that if it makes hinges move easily then it could do the same for the joints!

7 Leo Baekeland (1863-1944) discovered a new plastic through a chaotic accident. He made some fascinating chemical blobs by mixing phenol and formaldehyde. The blobs were a new kind of plastic – Bakelite. Mind you, legend has it he made the same discovery by spilling formaldehyde on his cheese sandwich!

8 *Dyes* made from chemicals in coal were discovered accidentally in 1856 by a young whiz-kid – William Perkin (1837-1907).

A colourful character

1. When Perkin was twelve a friend showed him some chemistry experiments.

THE POSSIBILITY OF NEW DISCOVERIES IMPRESSED ME VERY MUCH.

2. Young William decided to try a few chemistry experiments and a few years later enrolled in the Royal College of Science.

ROYA
OF SC

REVOLTING BLACK SLUDGE

3. One Easter holiday he was doing chemistry homework in his dad's garden shed. He was trying to make the medical drug, quinine, using a coal tar chemical as raw material. The result was a revolting black sludge.

4. Many scientists would have given up at this point but Perkin was intrigued. So he added alcohol, and some lovely purple crystals appeared.

5. This type of purple was a brand new colour. Nothing like it had ever been seen before. So Perkin tried making the crystals into a dye. They turned out to be ideal for dying silk.

WHAT AN INTERESTING ELECTROMAGNETIC REFLECTION

6. Perkin sent a sample of dyed silk to a Scottish firm and received a letter in return.

Dear William

If your discovery does not make the goods too expensive, it is decidedly one of the most valuable that has come out for a long time.

Yours faithfully,
Pillars of Perth

CRIKEY!

What could be more encouraging?

7. Young William talked his dad into putting up the money for a factory to make the purple dye he called "Tyrian purple".

8. Mauve turned out to be popular and fashionable. Soon everyone wanted to wear it. It was even used for stamps.

9. William became so rich that he was able to retire at the ripe old age of 35. He built a new house complete with private lab.

10. In 1869 he invented a red dye but a German scientist had beaten him to this discovery by one day!

11. In 1906 a celebration was held to commemorate the discovery of mauve. It was attended by the world's most distinguished scientists and business tycoons. And the guest of honour was 68-year-old William Perkin.

12. Sadly Perkin died soon afterwards. The excitement had been too much for him!

Meanwhile scientists were experimenting with plastics to find more man-made substances. And making more discoveries . . . by accident.

Plastic fact file

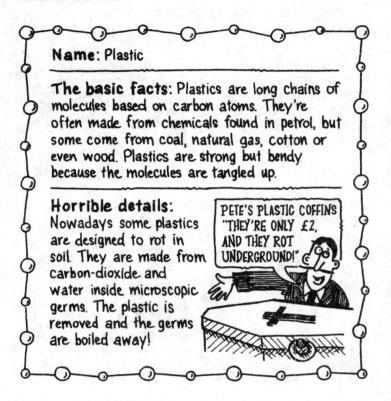

Name: Plastic

The basic facts: Plastics are long chains of molecules based on carbon atoms. They're often made from chemicals found in petrol, but some come from coal, natural gas, cotton or even wood. Plastics are strong but bendy because the molecules are tangled up.

Horrible details: Nowadays some plastics are designed to rot in soil. They are made from carbon-dioxide and water inside microscopic germs. The plastic is removed and the germs are boiled away!

PETE'S PLASTIC COFFINS "THEY'RE ONLY £2, AND THEY ROT UNDERGROUND!"

Fantastic plastics quiz

It's amazing the sheer variety of things that can be made from plastics. Which of these items do you think are made from plastics, and which sound too comical to be true?

1. DRUMS

2. BOOK COVERS

3. DRINK CARTONS

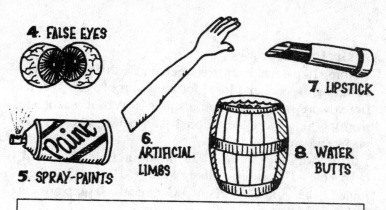

4. FALSE EYES

7. LIPSTICK

5. SPRAY-PAINTS

6. ARTIFICIAL LIMBS

8. WATER BUTTS

Answers: 1 TRUE – polyethylene. **2 FALSE** – a resin based lacquer stops the cover getting soggy if you spill a drink over it. Don't try this! Not on your Horrible Science book anyway! **3 TRUE 4 TRUE** – they contain acrylic so they don't break if they fall out of the eye socket! **5 TRUE** – they contain acrylics. **6 TRUE 7 FALSE 8 TRUE**

Chaotic chemical expressions

A chemist tells his best friend: My underwear is made from polyhexamethylene adipamide (polly-hexa-meeth-ile-ne adi-pam-ide).

Is this dangerous?

Answer: No – he's got nylon underpants.

Bet you never knew!

You're probably wearing plastic clothes! Many materials used in clothes such as polyester, acrylic, viscose and nylon are made from plastics. But nylon was discovered by accident, too. Here's what happened.

A stretchy story

Nothing like it had ever been seen on Earth before. It was as strong as steel and ideal for bullet-proof vests. Yet its fibres were no thicker than a spider's web. It was made from nothing more sensational than petrol, natural gas, water and air.

The story began in 1928 when a mild-mannered, bespectacled chemist called Wallace Hume Carothers joined the giant DuPont Chemicals company at Delaware, USA.

"Young man," said Company Vice-President Charles Stine. "I've got a special job for you. We're looking at ways to make silk from minerals."

Most of us would say, "Yikes, that's a tall order!" But Corothers looked thoughtful. "I'll need to look at polymers. I mean those stringy molecules that make silk so strong and flexible. I wonder if it's possible?"

"I guess the best way," said Carothers, "is to invent some new molecules."

"Well – that's your job, son. Just give it whatever it takes."

Carothers' lab was a chaotic maze of oddly-shaped flasks. There were tripods, jars filled with strange fluids and glass bottles with unreadable labels. But this is where he felt at home and where he made his great discovery.

After five years of research Carothers came up with his own substance – nylon. It was useless! Nylon was a clear plastic blob at the bottom of a test-tube. But it wouldn't melt unless you heated it to a high temperature. So how could it be made into fibres suitable for a fabric?

Carothers turned his attention to polyesters. One day Julian Hill, one of Carothers' assistants, was mucking about with some polyester in a test-tube. He was amazed to find that he could pull strands of it out on a rod – like gungey mozzarella cheese on a cooked pizza.

'Let's wait till the boss goes out,' he told the others. 'I wanna try a little test.'

They pulled the stringy polyester as far they could. It must have been a strange sight as they managed to stretch it several metres down a corridor.

But this process locked the polyester molecules into place to form strong fibres. Maybe they could do the same for nylon? Yes, they certainly could.

This dramatic breakthrough made it possible to create amazing new fabrics. Carothers' reaction when he got back wasn't recorded but he might well have said, "It's good to see you're working at full stretch. Ha ha!"

Nylon stockings were launched at the World Trade Fair in 1938. A female audience heard Charles Stine declare, "It's the first man-made organic textile fibre ... yet it's more elastic than any common natural fibres."

And the best news of all: nylon was going to be a lot cheaper than silk so more people could afford it. The audience were delighted and erupted into wild applause. They shouted and cheered until the ceiling shook. But Carothers wasn't there to see it...

A fatal finale
In 1936 he had fallen into despair following the death of his sister. The following year he took his own life with a dose of the deadly poison cyanide. He was only 41 years old.

More man-made marvels
Within a few years the world would be at war and nylon

was to prove itself a vital war-winning material. It was used to make countless parachutes and the used parachutes were then recycled to make stockings.

Nowadays, nylon is used to make not only stockings but everything from ropes and carpets to toothbrush bristles. Yet nylon is just one of hundreds of man-made substances. From A-Z they range from acrylic paints and zinc oxide (particularly useful for treating nappy rash).

Funnily enough – all these chemicals have something in common. They're made from atoms – those pesky little things that make chemists curious. Yup – it's time to get down to basics.

YOU'RE ALL JUST
A LOAD OF
OLD ATOMS!

Awesome atoms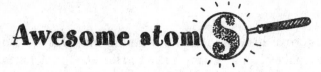

Atoms are awesome. Awesomely small that is. And awesomely important. After all, everything in the universe is made of them ... including you.

The incredible shrinking teacher

The machine stands ready. It's an awesome jumble of tubes and lasers all polished and ready for use. All that's required is a brave and perhaps foolhardy volunteer to venture into the unknown. This person will experience the awesome power of the incredible shrinking ray – and hopefully live to tell the tale.

The volunteer is ready. A person with nerves of steel. In the cause of Horrible Science she is about to embark on what might prove to be a one way trip. This heroic volunteer is none other than ... your science teacher.

HOORAY FOR MISS PERKINS!

She stands under the ray and seems to be disappearing. Soon she is no larger than a doll and she's still shrinking. In the blink of an eye she's become FIFTY times smaller. Now she's small enough to fit in your pocket! Then ... is it an ant or a gnat? No, it's your teacher – and she's smaller than ever. Now she's FIVE HUNDRED times smaller. Hey – where's she gone now?

The smallest object you can see is about one tenth of a millimetre long. Your teacher is now tinier than this. If you had a microscope you might still see your teacher if she was 400 times smaller. But already she's too small for this. Now she's smaller even than the tiniest droplet sprayed from an aerosol can – 1/50,000th of a mm! And that's pretty small!

Your incredible shrinking teacher is falling, plunging headlong towards a mass of balls churning like a stormy sea. Every ball looks like a tiny planet surrounded by clouds of chaos. She's arrived in the weird world of atoms.

It's a small world
- You can stretch one million atoms in a line and they'd just about cover the full stop at the end of this sentence.
- If you squeezed them a bit you'd fit one billion billion – that's 1,000,000,000,000,000,000 atoms – onto a pinhead.
- You can fit 600,000,000,000,000,000,000,000 (that's six hundred billion trillion) atoms into a thimble.

But if atoms are so small, how do we know they exist?

Chaotic chemists' hall of fame
Democritus (c. 460-370 BC) Nationality: Greek
This ancient Greek was known as "the laughing philosopher" – no one knows why. He was certainly laughed at by some people for suggesting the existence of atoms. Here's his idea...

CUT A PIECE OF CHEESE IN HALF ... CUT THE CHEESE IN HALF AGAIN AND AGAIN. EVENTUALLY YOU'LL GET A PIECE TOO SMALL TO CUT IN HALF. THAT'S AN ATOM!

In those days, few people imagined that atoms really existed so people poked fun at Democritus. But hundreds of years later he was proved right – so maybe he got the last laugh.

Bet you never knew!
Nowadays scientists can see atoms and even photograph them using a scanning tunnelling microscope. This brilliant bit of gizmo measures the electrical force between atoms at a single point. It produces amazing images that look strangely like table tennis balls!

Inside an awesome atom
Here's an interesting thought: imagine your incredible shrinking teacher ventures inside an atom. Here's what she sees.

1 An atom is a blob of matter called a nucleus surrounded by electrons. The electrons are tiny bits of electrical energy.

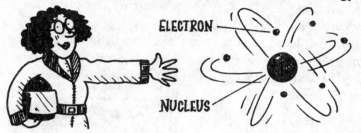

ELECTRON

NUCLEUS

2 Electrons zoom chaotically so that by the time you've spotted where they are they've moved somewhere else.

OOER!

3 Mind you, the electrons can't go just anywhere. They're found in layers known as orbits.

Dare you discover .... how to watch atoms in action?

You will need:

some water cooled in the fridge for two hours
food colouring
a large glass

All you do is:

1 Fill the glass half full with hot water.

2 Add a few drops of food colour and mix it up.

3 Fill the rest of the glass with the cold water. What happens?

a) Nothing at all. The bottom half of the water stays where it is.

b) The cold water at the top seems to be slipping down to mingle with the warm water in the bottom half.

c) The warm water seems to be moving upwards.

HMMM VERY INTERESTING

Answer: c) The warm water molecules are moving faster than the colder molecules. As they move apart they rise upwards. So you're seeing billions of atoms on the move.

The first problem for a chemist studying atoms is to work out how the atoms in a substance fit together. Now, the usual answer to this is to do lots of careful scientific experiments and then repeat them just to make sure they got it right. But one man had a different approach...

Choatic Chemists' Hall of Fame:
Friedrich Kekulé (1829-1896) Nationality: German
At school Kekulé was good at drawing and he studied to be an architect. One day he happened to attend a murder trial. Young Kekulé was enthralled by the gruesome

scientific evidence and surprised to find it wasn't laughed out of court. So Kekulé decided to train as a scientist so he could find out more about this scintillating subject. That's how he came to be in London in 1854.

A Dream Discovery

1. 1854. Kekulé was kipping on a double-decker bus.

2. All of a sudden he saw atoms dancing about.

3. Then he woke up.

4. But the dream had given him a nifty idea.

5. He decided to make model atoms using little balls joined by sticks.

THIS IS FUN!

That's how he figured out how some atoms can join together more easily than others to make new chemicals. It opened up a whole new field of chemistry. And all because of a dream!

6. 1863 Ghent, Belgium. Kekulé had another dream. He'd been writing a book whilst suffering a nasty dose of flu.

7. But he was also worrying about a tricky chemistry problem.

8. He dozed off and dreamt about snakes. Well, why not?

Benzene = a chemical in coal = 12 atoms. How are they arranged?

9. One of the snakes bit its own tail.

10. Kekulé awoke with a bright idea.

BENZENE IS RING-SHAPED

218

11. But many people thought this was a daft idea . . .

DREAM ON KEKULÉ!

It took years of patient experiments before Kekulé was certain his dream was correct. Benzene was indeed a ring of atoms. This dream discovery made it possible to develop new chemical dyes and thousands of other useful substances.

A DREAM COME TRUE!

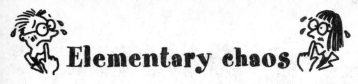

Elementary chaos

Atoms come in over one hundred varieties. These different varieties are known as elements. For years chemical knowledge was in chaos as confused chemists tried to classify these chemicals. The idea of elements was invented by a boring British scientist – John Dalton.

Chaotic chemists' hall of fame

John Dalton (1766-1844) Nationality: British

John Dalton wasn't exactly a laugh-a-minute kind of bloke. He would drone on non-stop for hours about science, science and more science. And if that reminds you of a science teacher you know, you won't be too amazed to learn that John was a science teacher, too. They really did start young in those days. John was only 12 when he started teaching.

BORING INDEED! YOU CAN STAY BEHIND AND SHARPEN THE QUILLS

Like most other scientists, John knew that water could be broken down into hydrogen and oxygen. But those chemicals couldn't be broken down further. So he called them "elements" and said that each was a type of atom. People poked fun at John. But they were soon laughing on the other side of the faces. Scientists found that their experiments proved John right. He became famous and now there's even a statue of him.

ALWAYS KNEW I WAS RIGHT!

Chaotic chemical elements

There are over 90 elements on Earth. Scientists have also created new elements out of tiny bits of matter. But these have the rather irritating habit of falling apart after a second. Here's your very own chaotic guide to elements that don't do this.

CHAOTIC ELEMENTS SPOTTER'S GUIDE

Name of element:
ALUMINIUM

Where found: in soil and rocks

Crucial characteristics: a light and useful metal. It's used to make tank armour, saucepans, kitchen foil and folding chairs. You can even make clothes out of it!

HATS TOO

Name of element:
CARBON

Where found: in diamonds, benzene, coal and the "lead" in your pencil.

Crucial characteristics: the most common atom in the human body, which is a bit weird, because people don't look anything like lumps of coal.

I DO

Name of element:
LEAD

Where found: This isn't the lead in your pencil. Real lead is a grey metal often found on old church roofs.

Crucial characteristics: it's quite a nasty poison if you happened to eat it by mistake. It's also very heavy so don't go dropping it on your teacher's toe.

Name of element:
CALCIUM

Where found: milk, chalk and marble and also in bones and the plaster used to set broken bones.

Crucial characteristics: if you burn calcium it gives off a lovely red flame. But that's no excuse for setting fire to your teacher's plastered toe!

OOH LOVELY!

Name of element:
CHLORINE

Where found: in salt, sea water and rock salt.

Crucial characteristics: it's very good for killing germs, but not very nice if it gets up your nose.

Name of element:
COPPER

Where found: in rocks under the ground.

Crucial characteristics: lots of uses including electrical wires and the rivets that hold your jeans together. Air pollution caused by cars and industry causes a chemical reaction that turns copper green That's why the copper plated Statue of Liberty in New York looks a bit sea-sick.

GET ME A BUCKET

Name of element: GOLD

Where found: in rocks under the ground.

Crucial characteristics: gold is good to make into jewellery – that's why people drape it round their necks. It's also worth lots of dosh.

Name of element: HELIUM

Where found: in the air

Crucial characteristics: used to fill balloons. It's lighter than air so the balloons float skywards. Breathing helium makes your voice sound like Mickey Mouse. This happens because your voice passes faster through helium than ordinary air. So it sounds higher and squeakier!

Name of element: HYDROGEN

Where found: it's the most common element. Stars such as the sun are made of hydrogen. So is 97 per cent of the known universe.

Crucial characteristics: hydrogen is also the lightest element so it floats upwards. This was why hydrogen gas was once used in balloons. It's also burnt as a rocket fuel. Hydrogen sulphide is a gas that stinks of rotten eggs. But don't confuse it with a stink bomb – it's poisonous.

Name of element: IRON

Where found: much of the earth is made of iron. You find it in rocks and the soil.

Crucial characteristics: you can use iron to make railings. It's also found in the chemical that gives blood its tasteful red colour.

Name of element: OXYGEN

Where found: it's the most common element on Planet Earth.

Crucial characteristics: it's really lucky that over one fifth of the atoms in the air are oxygen. Without them we'd be more than a little bit dead. Some people think that if they breathe pure oxygen they'll live longer. They must be confused because scientists believe that breathing too much oxygen is bad for you. They say it increases the pressure of the blood to dangerous levels.

Name of element: PLUTONIUM

Where found: it's found in nuclear reactors but nowhere else in nature.

Crucial characteristics: Plutonium is incredibly poisonous. It looks like metal but it turns green in the air. And damp air makes it catch fire! The man who discovered plutonium in 1940 kept a lump of it in a matchbox. Weird.

Name of element: SILVER

Where found: in underground rocks.

Crucial characteristics: a really useful shiny metal much prized for dangling around the neck, making the shiny backs of mirrors and really posh cutlery. In the last 50 years people have lost 100,000 tonnes of silver coins. Where have they all got to? That's what I'd like to know.

I'VE NO IDEA – HONEST!

Name of element: SULPHUR

Where found: sulphur is a smelly yellow chemical spat out of volcanoes in choking clouds.

Crucial characteristics: at one time it was known as brimstone and mixed with treacle. It was used as a medicine for children. The medicine tasted disgusting so it was probably spat out by the choking children too.

Odd elements quiz

Some of the more obscure elements are ever so odd. Which of these are too strange to be true?

TRUE or FALSE

1 The element phosphorous was discovered by an alchemist whilst he was examining the contents of his own urine.

2 The elements yttrium, erbium, terbium and ytterbium are all named after a quarry in Sweden.

3 The element dysprosium was discovered in 1886. The Greek name means "really smelly".

4 The element selenium was discovered by the Swedish scientist Berzelius. Sadly, he didn't realize it was poisonous until it poisoned him!

5 The element cadmium was discovered when it accidentally got into a bottle of medicine.

6 The element krypton was named after the planet that Superman comes from.

7 The scientist who discovered beryllium named it after his wife – Beryl.

8 The element Astatine is so rare that if you searched the entire world you'd only find 0.16 grammes of it.

9 Technetium was first found in caterpillar droppings.

10 Lutetium is named after the ancient Roman name for Paris.

Bet you never knew!

You can find all the different elements in the clever Periodic Table invented by Russian chemist Dmitri Mendeleyev (1834-1907). Here's how it works:

1 Elements are grouped according to the number of electrons in their outer orbits.

2 The elements in each group behave in similar ways when mixed with other chemicals.

Chaotic chemists' hall of fame:

Dmitri Mendeleyev (1834-1907) Nationality: Russian
Other scientists had difficulties. But Mendeleyev lived a real-life soap opera. His father was a teacher who went blind. His mother ran the family glass factory and brought up 14 children. But when Dmitri was 14 the factory burnt down.

Dmitri went to St Petersburg to study chemistry. He discovered the Periodic Table by writing the elements on cards and arranging them as in his favourite card game – Patience. In 1955 element 101 was named mendelevium in his honour. So Dmitri ended up in his own Table!

IT LOOKS VERY COMPLICATED

YES, IT DID REQUIRE SOME PATIENCE.

The complicated bit

So that's it. All you need to know is the Periodic Table and which elements join together. Simple, really? Er – no. Just to add a little chaos – chemicals are always changing and getting mixed up. Confused? You soon will be. See you in the next chapter!

CAN I HAVE SOME WATER, MUM?

WOULD YOU LIKE IT AS ICE, LIQUID, OR GAS, DEAR?

chaotic chemical changes

Everything changes – this fact is so well known it's a cliché. But WHY exactly do things change? Well, with chemicals it's mainly due to the effects of heat or cold. This can result in a few chaotic chemical mix-ups.

Bet you never knew!

You might think that water is runny, iron is solid, and oxygen is a gas. Wrong, wrong and WRONG again! In fact ANY chemical can be a solid, a liquid or a gas. It just depends on how hot the chemical is at the time. Below 0°C (32°F) water is the solid object we call ice. Above that temperature water turns into ... well ... water and above 100°C (212°F) water boils and turns into a gas – you'd probably call it steam.

Solid secrets

Have you ever wondered why some solid objects are bendy and others are very tough? Well, have you ever pondered why your auntie's best china is always breaking and why her rock cakes are ... just like rocks? Here's the answer.

- In every solid object the atoms are bonded together. But what's important is the way the atoms are arranged.
- If they're in stretchy strings the object will be stretchy like an elastic band. You can squash them together quite easily.

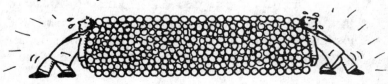

- In very hard materials such as diamonds the atoms are arranged in a very tight and very strong framework.

- In softer materials such as graphite – pencil lead – the atoms are arranged in loose layers that rub off easily when you write.

- In china the atoms are closely packed and joined tightly together. But if just one atomic join breaks the china will crack!

- In a metal the atoms are surrounded by a crowd of jostling electrons. (They're a bit like teachers in a playground at break-time.) The electrical force of the electrons keeps the atoms in place. But each atom can move a bit and that's why you can bend metal – if you're very strong!

GO ON, IT'S EASY!

Melting moments

Here are some impressive facts about melting and freezing water.

1 In Northern Canada some lakes freeze solid. The freezing starts with a single ice-crystal that grows and grows. So each frozen lake becomes a giant ice-crystal.

2 As water freezes it expands and crushes anything it traps with a force of 140 kg per square cm (42 stone per square inch). That's enough to sink a ship or crush a man to death!

3 You get snow and hail when water molecules join and freeze in the sky. Hailstones occur when lumps of ice swirl around in a cold cloud getting larger and larger. The largest hailstone ever was 19 cm (7 ½ inches) across and fell on Kansas in 1970.

OW!

4 You can make snowballs because snow is partly melted ice and slushy so you can squash the snow together. If it's really cold as in the Antarctic, the snow is hard and powdery.

So you can't have a snowball fight at the South Pole.

5 Here's what happens when you melt ice... When they are stuck together as ice the water molecules are fairly still although they do wobble a bit.

6 It's only when a chemical is really cold that the molecules stop moving completely. This temperature is -273.15°C (-459.67°F), absolute zero.

7 As ice melts the molecules take in heat energy and wobble about more and more. Then they wobble free and start floating around.

WOBBLING MOLECULE

MELTING ICE CUBE

YIPPEE!

FREE AT LAST!

8 As they heat up even more, they move faster and faster until they take a flying leap into the air and become a gas.

Bet you never knew!

1 Different chemicals melt and turn into gases at different temperatures. It's all to do with the bonds between atoms in the chemical. If these bonds are strong you need loads of heat energy to break them apart. So their melting point is higher.

2 All gases need to be very cold before they become liquids. To make liquid oxygen you need to cool it to -188.191°C (-306.74°F). And to make solid oxygen it needs to be a very chilly -218.792°C (-361.83°F)! Luckily, our weather isn't that cold or we'd have nothing to breathe. And that would cause chaos!

Test your teacher

Of course, anything can be a liquid – if it's the right temperature. Terrorize your teacher with this terribly tricky test.

1 Over hundreds of years glass sinks slowly to the bottom of a window frame. Does that make glass a liquid or solid?

2 The black displays that you get in some calculators are made out of crystals – are they a liquid or solid?

3 Is school custard a liquid or a solid?

NOT SURE – I'LL CHEW IT OVER

4 If you cool helium gas to -271°C (-455°F) it can be poured and it even climbs up the sides of a beaker. Is it liquid or solid?

Answers: 1 It's a liquid! **2** Trick question. They're somewhere in-between. These are special crystals that don't melt when heated so they're solid even when they ought to be a liquid! **3** It's a liquid called a colloid – that's a liquid with lots of little oily drops in. Yuck! One mark for colloid, half a mark for liquid and an upset tummy if it's solid. **4** Another trick question. It's a supercool liquid which explains why it acts rather oddly.

Mixed-up mixtures

Much of our planet is made up of mixed-up chemicals. Take a breath of air. In one gulp you'll get a chaotic combination of oxygen, nitrogen and hydrogen and a few other gases thrown in for good measure. All these atoms are completely mixed up, but guess what? The funny thing is that nothing happens, there's no reaction between them, so you don't notice them all.

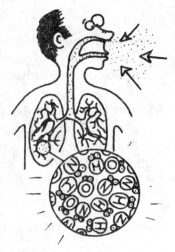

When you mix two gases or two liquids, the atoms of each chemical often spread out until they are thoroughly mixed. But some mixtures don't mix properly.

If a liquid is heavier than water it may sink to the bottom of a glass of water and not mix with it at all. Try out this chaotic chemical cocktail...

You will need:
a tall glass
water (adding a few drops of food colouring might make it more interesting)
oil
syrup (in roughly equal amounts)
umbrella (optional)
straw (optional)

All you do is:
1 Pour a similar amount of each of the three liquids into the glass.
2 Sit around and wait for something to happen.
3 Check your answer against these three possibles...

a) the liquids all mix together.

b) the water stays at the top, the oil sinks to the middle and the syrup to the bottom.

c) the oil rises to the top, the water stays in the middle and the syrup sinks to the bottom.

Answer: c) Unless you've gone chaotically wrong somewhere.

Bet you never knew!

If you mix up a solid substance with lots of water, the solid sometimes dissolves. But why does this happen? A water molecule is two hydrogen atoms joined to an oxygen atom. Funnily enough, the electrons of the hydrogen atoms have been stolen by the oxygen atom. This gives the hydrogen atoms a positive electrical force and the oxygen atom a negative force. Molecules innocently floating about in the water are caught between the forces and RIPPED APART! Sounds painful.

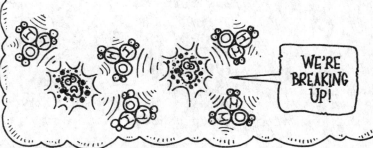

WE'RE BREAKING UP!

Un-mixing mixtures

Not only can you mix up chemicals, much of the time you can un-mix them too. For example, if a substance is mixed with water you can boil off the water and you're left with the original chemical. Talking about un-mixing things from water – one scientist had a very funny idea

235

about this. He was Germany's Fritz Haber and here's his story...

Chaotic chemists' hall of fame:

Fritz Haber (1868-1934) Nationality: German

Fritz Haber was a short and sharp-looking man and in old photographs he is always immaculately dressed. Born a merchant's son he dedicated his life to chemistry and the service of his country. Yes – Fritz was Germany's secret weapon.

Before the First World War (1914-1918) Fritz invented a new way to make a chemical called ammonia. This had good and bad results.

• The good news: the ammonia was used to make cheap fertilizers. Very handy for helping plants to grow.

• The bad news: it was used to make explosives. Very handy for blowing people up in the First World War.

Eventually the Germans lost the war. The country was in a mess and nearly penniless. And that's when Fritz had his funny idea.

Fritz goes gold hunting

If you really want to raise a few billion dollars don't wash your dad's car on a Sunday afternoon. Go prospecting for gold instead! There's gold in that there sea – millions of tons of clinky-clanky yellow stuff! Think about it ... 71 per cent of the Earth is covered by oceans with 97 per cent of all the world's water. Imagine millions of streams scouring gold from rocks and crevices and rivers washing it down to the sea!

But there's one teeny little problem. The gold is in tiny little atoms and grains. They're mixed up with trillions of tonnes of water, salts and all the seventy or so other chemicals you get dissolved in the sea.

In the previous fifty years no fewer than fifty scientists had come up with inventions for removing the gold. And they ALL failed!

But Fritz and his fellow scientists were all keen to have a go. So they chartered a luxury ocean liner called the *Hansa* and set sail in search of gold-rich seawater. The plan was to boil off the water and use other chemicals to separate the gold from the solid dregs.

But after three voyages and eight years they gave up. Here's the cause of their chaos. If you searched a billion buckets of seawater you'd find traces of gold in only 40 – if you were LUCKY! There's loads of gold in the sea but there's even more seawater. And getting the gold ain't worth the effort.

But that's not the last we'll hear of Fritz. He pops up rather nastily in the next chapter.

It's a gas!

Without gases there'd be chaos. We'd have nothing to breathe and balloons would fall out of the sky. Gases can be chaotic – especially when they poison people or explode! But they're interesting, too. Sometimes they're even funny – take nitrous oxide, for example, better known to you as laughing gas.

... MY CAT WAS RUN OVER

... THE CAR WAS STOLEN

... AND OUR HOUSE BURNT DOWN!

Gases fact file

Name: Gases

The basic facts: Gases are atoms or clumps of atoms that whiz about like tiny balls. You can feel the gas atoms in the air every time you go out in a wind.

Horrible details: Some gases are poisonous. (See next few pages for details.)

Stink bombs

Some chemists don't smell too good. This must be true otherwise they wouldn't produce such stinky substances. Any smell is caused by gas molecules which we sniff in the air. Now *you* can kick up a bit of a stink using...

There are 17,000 smells known to science but the worst are ethyl-mercaptan (e-thile-mare-cap-tan) and butyl seleno-mercaptan (bu-tile see-le-no-mare-cap-tan). Both gases pong like rotten cabbage, garlic, onions, burnt toast and sewer gas ALL MIXED TOGETHER! Phwoar!

But if you really want more whiff for your money there's always vanillaldehyde (van-nill-aldy-hyde). This chemical is made in a laboratory and it smells of vanilla. In fact, it's so smelly that just three ten-thousandths of a gram is enough to pong out an indoor sports stadium. Hope your vanilla-flavoured choc-ice is more delicately fragranced.

Dare you discover ... gas experiments?
1 Want to grab a bit of gas?
You will need:
a balloon

All you do is:
1 Blow up the balloon and pinch the end with your fingers.
2 Squeeze the balloon.
What happens?
a) As you squash more the balloon gets harder to squeeze.
b) As you squash more the balloon gets softer.
c) The balloon stays the same.

2 Make your own gas
You will need:
a narrow-necked bottle half-filled with water
a balloon (use the same one!)
2 alka-seltzer tablets.

All you do is:
1 Blow the balloon up and release the air a few times to make it softer.
2 Tilt the bottle on its side and place the tablets in the neck of the bottle.
3 Stretch the balloon over the neck of the bottle.
4 Allow the tablets to fall in the water.
What happens?

a) The balloon is sucked into the bottle.
b) There is a small explosion.
c) The balloon inflates slightly.

3 Bubble trouble

You will need:
a bottle of fizzy mineral water, lemonade or cola.

All you do is:
Give the bottle a really good shake for two minutes.
Slowly open the top and notice what happens.
a) Nothing
b) Loads of bubbles form and gas escapes.
c) Bubbles appear then sink to the bottom.

Answers: 1 a) Billions of gas atoms are squashed together. The harder you squeeze, the harder those atoms push back! **2 c)** The tablets react with water to make carbon dioxide gas. The molecules of this gas are made from one carbon and two oxygen atoms joined together. **3 b)** The fizz comes from carbon dioxide bubbles. The gas is dissolved in water under pressure. Removing the top reduces pressure and allows bubbles to form.

Bet you never knew!
Just as in experiment 3 gas bubbles form in the blood of deep sea divers as they surface. The "bends" as they are called can have fatal results! To prevent this, divers spend time in a pressurized chamber so their bodies get used to the change in pressure.

What a gas!

The air is mainly made of nitrogen. Some plants use this to help them grow though it doesn't do much for us. But the oxygen and carbon dioxide in the air are worth gassing about.

Chaotic chemists' hall of fame:

Joseph Priestley (1733-1804) Nationality: British
Priestley's friend Sir Humphry Davy said:

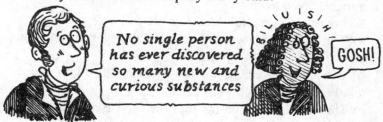

> *No single person has ever discovered so many new and curious substances*

GOSH!

(Not since the first scientific analysis of school dinners anyway.) Joe could speak nine languages but he was useless at maths. In the 1790s Priestley disagreed with the Government and his political enemies sent a mob to smash up his lab. The shaken scientist did a runner to the USA. Could you think like Priestley? Try explaining the results of one of his famous experiments.

A load of hot air

1 In 1674 scientist John Mayow put a mouse in a jar with a candle.

243

2 The mouse fainted as the candle burnt out.

3 In 1771 Priestley burnt a candle in a jar until the flame went out. Then he added a sprig of mint to the jar.

4 The plant stayed healthy.

5 A few months later Priestley added a mouse. This time the mouse stayed awake.

6 Finally the scientist added a candle in the jar again. The candle burnt normally, the plant stayed healthy and the mouse stayed awake.

So how do you explain these results?

a) The mouse produced a gas that the plant used. The candle also used this gas.

b) The plant used a gas made by the candle and produced another gas that the mouse used.

c) The candle made a gas that the mouse and the plant both used.

Answer: b) Yes – the plant used the carbon dioxide to make food and produced oxygen so that the mouse could breathe.

In 1774 Priestley heated mercuric oxide to make a colourless non-smelly gas. He put this gas in a jar and added a mouse. The mouse seemed happy and relaxed. So Priestley sniffed the gas.

AHA! THE RODENT SEEMETH CONTENTED

SNIFF SNIFF

Which gas was it?

a) The gas produced by the plant.

b) The gas produced by the candle.

c) The gas produced by the mouse.

Bet you never knew!
Joseph Priestley invented fizzy drinks. He put together a home-made machine from a washing tub and a few wine glasses and bubbled carbon dioxide through water. The water tasted fizzy and you could flavour it with fruit juices. But Priestley stored the gas in a pig's bladder and funnily enough some people complained that the drink had a "piggy" flavour.

Trick question for your teacher.
Who discovered oxygen – Priestley or Lavoisier?

Chaotic chemists' hall of fame:
Karl Scheele (1746-1786) Nationality: Swedish
Karl Scheele discovered new chemicals such as oxygen, chlorine and nitrogen. But life wasn't much of a gas for

this sad scientist. Owing to a publishing mix-up the book describing his discoveries wasn't printed for 28 years! Meanwhile, other chemists had discovered the same chemicals. And to make matters even worse, Scheele died after being poisoned by a chemical he discovered but never got the credit for!

A mad machine

Meanwhile Lavoisier investigated hydrogen gas. This lighter than air chemical was ideal for filling balloons so they floated upwards. But there was one problem – hydrogen burns easily. In 1783 French balloon pioneer Pilâtre de Roziers tried to fly this chaotic machine. Can you guess what happened?

Answer: The hydrogen balloon caught fire and exploded. The barmy balloonist was killed.

The last laugh

Sir Humphry Davy (1778-1829) was 19 when he discovered laughing gas, or nitrous oxide as the chemists call it. He thought there was something funny about the gas when he sniffed it. And he felt so good that he burst into gales of laughter.

Laughing gas shows became a popular form of entertainment. You could see people sniffing the gas and making fools of themselves. In 1839 a chemist described how people breathed the gas out of pigs' bladders:

> Some jumped over tables and chairs, some were bent on making speeches, some were very much inclined to fight . . . As to the laughing, I think it was chiefly confined to the lookers-on.

And the funny thing was that people under the influence of the gas didn't seem to feel any pain.

The dabbling dentist

Ambitious American dentist Horace Wells (1815-1848) experimented unsuccessfully with laughing gas as a way of knocking people out for operations. Later he went mad and killed himself. Meanwhile his former partner William T. Morton the proud owner of a false teeth factory, was experimenting with another chemical – ether.

Following the advice of a professor called Charles Jackson, Morton tested the gas on his pet dog and then on himself. Mind you, I don't suppose he noticed that he'd knocked himself out. Next he tried it on a patient. Success! Sadly, this story has a painful ending. Ether is quite cheap and easy to make. So to make money Morton said he'd invented a brand new substance.

He coloured the ether pink and added perfumes to it so no one would recognize it. Then he sold the bottles to doctors at ludicrous prices. He thought he'd be laughing all the way to the bank. But when the doctors found out they'd been cheated, they lost all confidence in Morton.

Morton exchanged a lot of hot air in his arguments with Charles Jackson over who had discovered ether. One day the inventor read a magazine article crediting Jackson with the discovery. He was so cross he had a fit and died. Meanwhile, Jackson had been acting rather oddly. After a visit to Morton's grave he went mad and had to be locked up.

In the last fifty years laughing gas has come back into

fashion. It has been extensively used to knock people out before operations.

So I suppose Horace Wells got the last laugh.

And if you think this story sounds chaotic, wait till you get wind of these nasty niffs...

The most horrible gas competition

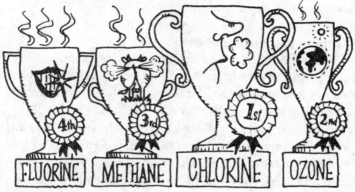

Fourth prize

Fluorine Five scientists tried to make this gas – all were poisoned. Eventually French scientist Henri Moissan (1852-1907) succeeded using platinum equipment. Platinum is one of the few materials fluorine doesn't dissolve.

Nowadays, tiny safe amounts of fluorine atoms are found in the chemicals called fluorides in toothpaste that help protect teeth from decay. That's OK, but too much fluoride actually discolours teeth.

Third prize

Methane gas bubbling from marshes catches fire to make the ghostly lights called will-o'-the-wisps or jack-o'-lantern. You'll also find methane in cows' farts (and humans') – *and* the gas that people use for cooking. It's true!

249

Second prize – runner up
Ozone gas molecules are formed by three oxygen atoms joined together. They smell of new-mown hay and were discovered when a scientist noticed a funny pong in his lab.

Ozone kills germs. It also kills people if they breathe too much of it. Luckily most ozone is 25 km (16 miles) up in the air where it forms a useful barrier against the sun's harmful rays.

Winner (just nosing ahead)
Chlorine Pollution by gases containing chlorine caused a hole in the ozone layer over Antarctica. The gap is as deep as Mount Everest and as big as North America and it's getting bigger all the time.

But this horrible yellow-green gas has been causing problems for centuries. Over 600 years ago an alchemist bubbled chlorine though water and said it was good for salad dressings. WRONG. Chlorine is horribly poisonous.

WOW! IT'S TURNED BLUE – I WONDER WHAT IT TASTES LIKE

In the First World War German scientist Fritz Haber developed chlorine gas as a horrible weapon of war...

A breath of air
"Tell me about it," Billy pleaded.

Arthur McAllsop hunched his shoulders against the cold drizzle and shook his head. "I've told you son – it's not a nice story."

"You said you'd look after me."

"Yeah, I did. Listen son, just keep your head down and you'll be alright."

"Well, I need to know about it. Can't have been too bad – you're still here aren't you?"

A flare cut through the night. Billy blinked in the sudden blaze of light. He looked so young – just sixteen and his first time away from home. Must have lied about his age.

Arthur sighed. There was nothing for it. The boy would find out soon enough.

"We were near Ypres, I expect you've heard of the fights there in 1915. Well, it was a quiet sort of day – warm for April. Nothing much to bother us all day. We were having a nice cup of tea when it happened."

"What happened?" asked Billy.

"Gas," said Arthur. "The gas attack. It was like a yellow fog rolling down. Well, luckily the wind blew the worst of it away. We didn't have gas masks then."

"Did you get gassed?"

"Only a bit. It was like a horrible sore throat and I couldn't stop coughing. But I was lucky – I was still alive."

"That night it poured with rain. The shelling didn't let up. Not for one moment. Chaos. You couldn't hear yourself talk. We had nothing to eat, no sleep. After we came out of the line everything was a mess. The gas had turned all the grass yellow. And there were no birds in the trees."

There was a long silence. It was a quiet night and if you listened hard you could hear voices from the enemy trenches. Orders in a foreign language. Then came a crack of rifle fire and the whine of a stray bullet.

"Arthur, you don't think they'd use gas on us?"

Both men sniffed the air. The trench smelled of mouldy earth. Muddy water squelched on the duckboards beneath their army boots.

"No Billy – we'll be alright. They put the gas in shells now. They don't blow up but they do go plop! So if one plops you'd better put your gas mask on double-quick!"

It was getting lighter and a chill dawn breeze set the barbed wire twanging. Soon it would be time to stand to – then they could eat breakfast.

The soldiers heard the approaching shell. It whistled through the air like a train getting louder and louder. They both crouched, instinctively ducking their heads.

Waiting for the bang that never came. Instead the shell fell in the mud of No Man's Land with a gentle plop.

Billy turned white.

"Gas," he cried in a choking voice. "GAS!"

In seconds the word was passed down the line. Half-awakened soldiers groaned and cursed – fumbling with the clumsy gas masks they wore around their necks.

Only one man did nothing. A man who had already seen the worst of gas warfare and knew what to expect.

"Don't be silly, Billy!" cried Arthur McAllsop. "It's a dud shell. Gas shells don't whistle like that!"

Bet you never knew!
1 By the end of the First World War more then 125,000 tonnes (123,025 tons) of gas had been released by both the British and the Germans.
2 The first gas masks were rifle cleaning cloths soaked in urine (the water in the urine was supposed to absorb the gas). Yuck!
3 Eventually the soldiers were given gas masks that absorbed the gas in layers of charcoal.
4 In 1975 Dr Buddy Lapidus used this idea to invent odour-eating insoles. The charcoal eats up nasty smelly foot odour like a little gas mask!

But gases aren't the only deadly chemicals. Metals make murderous weapons, too.

Marvellous murderous metals

What's hard, shiny and doesn't bounce when it hits the floor? No, it's not your teacher's bald head, although it could be – it's a metal! Where would we be without metals? Think of the chaos it would cause. We'd have no coins, cars or computers for a start. But then we'd also have less in the way of murderous weapons. Let's face the facts...

Metals fact file

Name: Metals

The basic facts: In a metal the atoms aren't actually joined together - they're surrounded by a crowd of electrons. This allows you to bend metals and stretch them into wires.

Horrible details: Some metals have horrible habits. Two called rubidium and caesium must be kept away from water to stop them exploding!

HOW MUCH FOR THE UMBRELLA?

RUBIDIUM

CAESIUM

But metals have many amazing secrets too!

Marvellous metal facts

1 Some metals can float on water – for example, sodium does until it reacts with the water to make hydrogen gas.

2 Mercury is a metal that is actually a liquid at room temperature. You can see it in your thermometer. As the mercury heats up, it expands up the scale. Mind you – one Russian winter the thermometers all froze at -38°C. If your school ever gets that cold it's time to go home!

3 Gallium melts so easily that if you put some in your hand it slowly collapses into a greasy puddle!

4 Tantalum is a rare grey metal used to make plates that cover holes in the skull.

5 Nowadays, platinum is more valuable than gold. But the funny thing is that in the sixteenth century the Spanish government thought the metal could be made into fake coins. So they dumped their entire stock of platinum in the sea!

6 In 1800 William H. Wollaston (1766-1828) invented a way to re-shape platinum into long threads so it could be made into new shapes. The cunning chemist was raking in cash like crazy from his invention and made sure no one else found out. The secret was revealed after he died. Well – he didn't need the money any more!

7 Titanium is a metal that doesn't melt easily. This is good for making fast aircraft because their wings get very hot due to air molecules rubbing over them at high speed.

8 Scientists have suggested making artificial legs out of titanium. At least they won't buckle under in the heat of the sun!

Sensational silver

Silver is so widely used it's difficult to believe that anything could be so useful. Which of these silver adverts are too stupid to be true?

a PROBLEMS WITH PAINFUL JOINTS?
Take these real silver pills. Genuine cure promised.

b Are your knuckle joints wearing out? Replace them today with this lovely silver set. Invest for the future!

c Jet engine for sale – genuine solid silver bits in it.

d Problems with germs?
A silver water tank kills germs and keeps your water fresher for longer.

e LOVELY SILVER SOLAR PANELS.
Now you can live on the sunny side of the street.

f BURNS ARE A PAIN!
Take this soothing silver lotion. Guaranteed healing!

Answers: All are TRUE except b)!

Amazing aluminium

Apart from silver, aluminium is one of the most useful metals known to man. But aluminium was once amazingly difficult and expensive to make. The French Emperor Napoleon III had his cutlery and baby's rattle made out of aluminium just to show how wealthy he was!

Chaotic chemists' hall of fame:

Charles M. Hall (1863-1914) Nationality: American
Paul L.T. Héroult (1863-1914) Nationality: French
One day Charlie heard his teacher say,

So the go-getting young American decided to have a go. Soon he was hard at work on his main piece of equipment . . . a grotty old gas stove in a woodshed.

Against all the odds – Charlie succeeded! The trick is to dissolve aluminium-rich bauxite in a chemical called cryolite. Amazingly this discovery was made at the same time by Frenchman Paul Héroult. Both inventors were exactly the same age and both worked in similarly chaotic chemistry labs! And here's the really bizarre bit. They were born and died in the same year too! Aluminium may be amazing, but it's not...

As good as gold

Yes – GOLD. It's the stuff that dreams are made of. Royal crowns, pirate treasure, ancient coins. For thousands of years men have fought, struggled and died to get their mits on this magical metal. And sometimes they've made complete fools of themselves...

Fool's Gold

Sir Martin Frobisher (1537?-1596) was nobody's fool. The tough-talking Yorkshireman was everyone's idea of an explorer – brave, weather-beaten and determined.

In 1576 Frobisher sailed off in search of a sea route to Asia across the north of Canada. Sir Martin didn't find the fabled route but he did visit the icy wilderness of Baffin Island. And there he made a stunning discovery.

It was a lump of rock that glittered in the chilly northern sun! Back in England an alchemist confirmed it, "Yup – it's gold." Chaos soon ensued because everyone wanted to grab a share.

IT'S COLD... IT'S OLD... IT'S GOLD!!!

The next year, Frobisher returned to the island with a larger expedition. It was no picnic – they braved icebergs and gales that could tear a ship to pieces. On land there were polar bears strong enough to kill a man with a single blow. But it was worth the danger. Working with picks in the freezing cold, they hacked away 180 tonnes of the golden rock.

The following year Frobisher headed an armada full of excited adventurers. This time the ships returned laden with an incredible 1,180 tonnes of the glittering prize. It was worth a fortune – enough to make them rich beyond their wildest dreams. Or so they reckoned...

Then the bubble burst. There was no gold on Baffin Island. It was just iron pyrite – a common-as-muck compound of iron ore and sulphur that you can find anywhere. Some unkind people called it "fool's gold". Sir Martin and his crew became a laughing stock.

Would you have been fooled by iron pyrite? Here are a few tips to make sure you get the right stuff.

Become a Gold Prospector
1 Panning for gold
Swirl a load of sand and water in a pan. Carefully swill the water and floating sand from the pan. Any gold will settle to the bottom of the pan as golden grains or nuggets.
2 Testing for gold
Scrape your golden nugget on a dark rock called a touchstone. If it leaves a streak of gold it's genuine.

3 Dig a gold mine
It takes time to dig your own mine. Some mines are thousands of metres deep so don't dig into your garden unless you're sure there's real gold lurking in the rocks beneath. You have got real gold in the rocks beneath your garden? OK, then, here's how to get at it.

Getting the gold . . .

1 You'll need to spend a lot of money on machines, etc. One million pounds should cover it.

2 Smash thousands of tonnes of rock with heavy machines. Check every bit of rock to make sure you don't chuck away the golden nuggets by mistake. (You wouldn't see the funny side of this.)

3 Then smash them up in a giant cylinder filled with ball-bearings. (It's much quicker than using a potato masher.)

4 Mix the rock powder with the deadly poison cyanide plus water to make a slimy mess. (Don't try this in the living room.)

5 Leave the slime to settle in a tank. Then remove any bits of rock. Check for gold.

6 Add zinc dust to the slime. This separates out the cyanide from any gold there.

7 Melt the gold with a chemical called borax. The borax sticks to any unwanted chemicals and floats to the top of the mixture. Carefully skim this off.

8 A bit of further processing and you end up with a bar of 99.6% gold. It's as simple as that! (NOT)

Now you've gone to all this trouble to get gold, what do you do with it? Oddly enough, you might put it back underground – in a bank vault. That's where half the world's gold ends up!

> *Bet you never knew!*
> *Gold was used in medicines to kill off the lung disease, tuberculosis, but it poisoned the patients too. Yes, there's a mean side to metals. In fact, you could call them murderous.*

Murderous metal poisons

Lead is dangerous. Sixteenth-century ladies used white lead face powder to improve their complexions. After a few years the poison ruined their skin – it absorbed the lead and gave them blood poisoning. But the ladies didn't know why their skin was ruined so they used extra lead to cover up the damage!

But the most poisonous metal in the world is arsenic. Many years ago this substance was used to make fly papers. Flies stuck to the paper and came to a sticky end once the arsenic got to work. Unfortunately a few humans went the same way too.

Mind you, poison isn't the only way that metals can murder people. Metals make lethal weapons too.

Murderous metal weapons

1. The first iron weapons were made from meteorites that fell from outer space.

2. In 1500BC people worked out how to heat iron-ore to make metal, but it wasn't very strong.

3. Iron needed to be mixed with another metal before it was really strong. In 1200BC people first added carbon to iron to make it stronger.

ONE PORTION OF CARBON

4. Meanwhile soldiers fought with bronze swords. But they often bent in battle!

HA HA HA

5. Iron swords were much harder, sharper . . . and more deadly.

SWOOSH

And that wasn't all. There followed iron guns and iron cannon firing iron cannon balls. This led to more chaos on the battlefield and buckets of blood being spilt. And oddly enough, there's iron in blood too.

Chaotic chemical expressions

ARGHH!
HYDRATED IRON-OXIDES.
IT'S $Fe_2O_3H_2O$ AGAIN!

IS THIS THE END OF THE WORLD?

Answer: No. Her car's got a spot of rust.

A rotten reaction

One big problem with iron is that it joins up with oxygen atoms to make rust. That's right – rust is a compound of iron and oxygen atoms. And rusting is speeded up by water and salt. This is why rusty old ships sail the salty seas.

And rusting is just one of many rotten reactions.

RUST IS A MIXTURE OF IRON AND OXYGEN ATOMS – WATER AND SALT ACCELERATE THE PROCESS, BLAH BLAH...

SHUT UP AND KEEP BAILING MAN!

Rotten reactions

What have rusting and rotting got in common with photography? Give up? They're all based on chemical reactions. But what exactly is a chemical reaction?

Reactions fact file

Name: Chemical Reactions

The basic facts: A chemical reaction is when atoms join together – or joined-up atoms split apart so new chemicals appear.

Horrible details: Rusting isn't the only rotten reaction caused by oxygen. Oxygen mixed with butter or margarine over time makes them revoltingly rancid! It's enough to wipe the smile off anyone's face.

GAG SPLUTTER

Quick reactions

Normally, when atoms bump into one another they bounce apart again. But if they're moving fast they can stick together before they have a chance to rebound. The outer groups of electrons decide what happens next...
Sometimes atom kindly gives the other its electrons.

When this happens an electrical force sticks the atoms together like metal to a magnet. This is an ionic bond and it's more common in salts and other minerals.

Sometimes, the atoms share electrons. The electrons whiz round both atoms. When atoms join together like this it's called a covalent bond.

These bonds tend to form between non-metals – often gases or liquids. With both types of bond a new chemical is created.

Predictable reactions

So atoms bump together and decide to join up. It sounds
hit or miss doesn't it? But it isn't. Do you remember
Mendeleyev playing Patience in the chapter,
"Elementary chaos"? Thanks to Mendeleyev's Periodic
Table, scientists can predict what happens. It's so simple.
It just depends on the number of outer electrons an atom
has. If you have an adverse reaction to this, you shouldn't
try this puzzle.

Rotten reaction puzzle

Here are the atoms you'll be using to work out the puzzles.

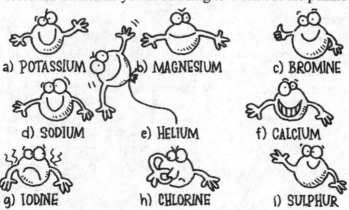

a) POTASSIUM b) MAGNESIUM c) BROMINE

d) SODIUM e) HELIUM f) CALCIUM

g) IODINE h) CHLORINE i) SULPHUR

First puzzle

How many outer electrons does each atom have? Read the clues below then work it out for all the atoms above.

Clues:

1 Sulphur has six electrons – that's three times more electrons than calcium. But between them they've enough to make a new chemical.

2 Helium has the same number of electrons as sulphur and calcium combined.

3 Magnesium has twice as many electrons as sodium and potassium.

4 Sodium and chlorine have enough electrons to make a chemical called sodium chloride. That's salt to you.

5 But sodium has only half as many electrons as calcium.

6 All the other atoms have one less electron than helium.

Second puzzle

For two chemicals to join they need a combined total of eight electrons in their outer orbits. Which atoms can join together to make new chemicals? Remember, they need a combined total of eight electrons in their outer orbits.

Answers: First puzzle a) 1 b) 2 c) 7 d) 1 e) 8 f) 2 g) 7 h) 7 i) 6
Second puzzle Potassium/sodium + bromine/iodine/chlorine • Magnesium/calcium + sulphur • Helium can't join with any other atom.

MY Cu + Ag No₃ HASN'T
BECOME Cu(NO₃) 2Ag
BOO HOO!

IS THIS FATAL?

Answer: No. His photos haven't come out.

Get the picture!

You might think these chemical reactions are a bit remote from everyday life. Surely you'd never normally have a hand in a reaction? But if you take a photograph you'll need a chemical reaction to get the picture!

1 The first photographers used light-sensitive silver chloride paper. Energy from light causes a reaction that turns the silver chloride black.

2 Light showed up as dark on the photograph. Dark patches showed up as white.

3 To be in a photo you had to sit still and wait for the chemical action to work. This could take hours and meanwhile you had to keep a totally straight face!

GOSH IS THAT THE TIME? NOW JUST STAY STILL FOR AN HOUR WHILE I HAVE MY LUNCH

4 Unfortunately the chemicals continued to react to light so you had to look at your photographs in the dark!

5 This problem was overcome when inventors discovered a chemical that removes silver chloride from the photograph.
6 Modern black and white film has quick light-reacting silver bromide salts. This means you can take action-photos.

7 Some of these salts are so sensitive to light you could take a photo from Earth of a candle flame on the Moon!

SAY CHEESE

Electrifying reactions

One incredibly useful type of reaction is electrolysis. It was developed by scientific superstar Michael Faraday.

Chaotic chemists' hall of fame:

Michael Faraday (1791-1867) Nationality: British
Michael had a tough childhood. His family were so poor that one day he was given a loaf of bread...

OH!

THAT'S ALL YOU'RE GETTING UNTIL NEXT WEEK!

He couldn't afford books but he got interested in science after reading books that he was supposed to be binding for a bookseller. He asked Sir Humphry Davy to take him on as an assistant. As luck would have it, Davy was temporarily blinded during a particularly dangerous experiment. So Faraday got the job.

WHAT A BIND!

Faraday investigated the process of electrolysis using different chemicals. Basically, you mix compounds with ionic bonds with water and run electricity through the solution. The atoms are pulled towards one or other of the two electrical terminals. The chemical gets torn apart!

Bet you never knew!
One use for electrolysis is in electroplating. You electrolyse a compound containing metal and a thin layer of the metal forms over an object. It's used to make silver-plated jewellery, for example. In 1891 sinister French surgeon, Dr Varlot, used the technique to cover a dead body in metal. The result of this revolting process was to wrap the body in a 1 mm layer of copper. He then put the gruesome object on display. I bet he got a few shocked reactions.

Quicker and slower reactions

Some reactions take a second – but others take millions of years. Luckily for chemists, many reactions are speeded up by heat. This makes atoms move a lot faster so they bump together more often. But you can slow down reactions by cooling. That's why food (and dead bodies) can be kept cold to prevent the reactions that make things go rotten.

Dare you discover ... how to stop a reaction using another reaction?

You will need:
an apple chopped into pieces
some lemon juice

All you do is:

1 Leave a piece of apple uncovered for a few hours and it goes brown. It's a reaction between chemicals in the apple and oxygen in the air just like rusting. It's starting to rot.
2 Try sprinkling some lemon juice over another piece of apple. What happens?

DON'T TOUCH MY EXPERIMENT MUM!

YUK!

FESTERING APPLE

a) The apple goes black.
b) The apple stays the same.
c) The apple dissolves.

Answer: b) The acid in the lemon juice reacts with metal atoms in the apple that would normally help to speed up the other reaction.

But acids have their gruesome side too. See the next chapter for the grisly details.

ACID DROP?

Appalling acids

They lurk in lemons and vinegar and tea leaves and even car batteries. Some of them have killer molecules that rip apart other nicer chemicals. It's appalling what they can get up to. Can you face the facts. . .?

Acids fact file

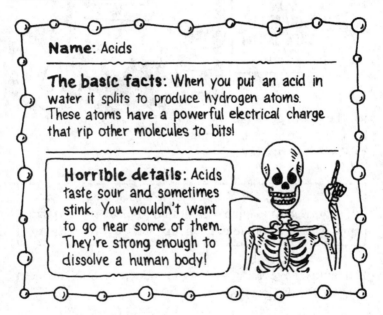

Name: Acids

The basic facts: When you put an acid in water it splits to produce hydrogen atoms. These atoms have a powerful electrical charge that rip other molecules to bits!

Horrible details: Acids taste sour and sometimes stink. You wouldn't want to go near some of them. They're strong enough to dissolve a human body!

But not every acid is quite so appalling. Sometimes they can even be useful...

Useful acid facts

1 Amino acids are molecules that join to make proteins. Most of your body is made of proteins.

2 Ascorbic acid is another name for Vitamin C. This

useful chemical is found in fresh fruit and prevents the deadly disease, scurvy. The vital vitamin was discovered by two different chemists and they spent the rest of their lives arguing over who was first!

3 Do you like the flavour of orange or lemon juice? Well, that's acid. Yes, citric acid helps make the taste of the juice.
4 Alginic (al-jin-ick) acid is found in seaweed. It's useful for keeping cakes moist and when added to bandages helps to stop bleeding! It's even used in ice-cream to stop the ingredients separating. You can amuse your friends by telling them their ice-cream started off as seaweed!

5 Salicylic (sallis-sill-ick) acid is used to make aspirin. Yes – the miracle pain-killer is an acid. It was first found in willow bark. People once chewed the wood to reduce fevers. Don't try this – it tastes disgusting.
6 Horribly useful acids were once used to produce leather. These tannic acids from acorns or poisonous hemlock bark killed the germs that made leather rot. The acids are also found in many other substances including tree bark

or even a cup of tea, but luckily they don't harm people. But other acids are completely useless.

Appalling acid rain

What do these places have in common – the Acropolis, Athens, St. Paul's Cathedral, London and the Lincoln Memorial, Washington? Give up? They're all being dissolved ... by RAIN! Industry and traffic produce sulphur dioxide gas. This makes rain more acid. In 1974 rain fell on Scotland that was as acid as lemon juice. That must have left people feeling rather sour.

Volcanoes make the problem worse. In 1982, the volcano El Chichin in Mexico belched out thousands of tonnes of acid gas!

Acid rain eats away at buildings old and new. Even your school is in danger! Oh well, every cloud has a silver lining.

It kills trees by the million.

It does terrible things to fish. They don't grow and the

acid dissolves their bones!

Acid rain doesn't dissolve people. But funnily enough, it can turn your hair green. It reacts with copper in water pipes to form copper sulphate, which causes the interesting colour change.

Chaotic chemical expressions

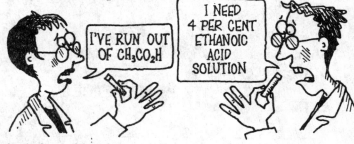

What's their problem?

Answer: No vinegar for their chips.

Dare you discover ... some simple solutions?
Dissolving a bone
You will need:

a stiff bone with no cracks in it. No need to go to too much trouble – a chicken bone will do.

vinegar

All you do is:

Cover the bone in vinegar and leave it for 12 hours.
What do you notice about the bone?

a) It's gone green.
b) It bends easily.
c) It's only half its original size.

Sour secrets
You will need:
15 drops of lemon juice
A cup of milk

All you do is:
Stir the ingredients together. What happens next?
a) The milk goes pale blue.
b) The milk gives off a disgusting smell.
c) The milk curdles.

Bottled egg
You will need:
a fresh egg
some vinegar
a glass
a bottle with a wide neck

HOW DO THEY DO THAT?

All you do is:
1 Soak the egg in the vinegar for two days. The egg will look the same but the shell will be thinner and softer.

2 You can carefully squeeze the egg into a bottle. Ask your friends to guess how you did it.

Bet you never knew!
You've got acid in your stomach. This fact was discovered by William Prout (1785-1850) in 1823. The hydrochloric acid kills germs and dissolves your food. So why doesn't it dissolve people too? Well the funny thing is – sometimes it does – that's when people get ulcers. The slimy stomach wall usually stops this happening but too much acid can cause indigestion.

Sinister sulphuric acid

It's oily, colourless and turns things to sludge, but it's got nothing to do with school dinners. It's sulphuric acid – a chemical so powerful that it has to be watered down before it can be used safely.

So why bother making sulphuric acid? Well, it does have its uses. For example, you can use it to make fertilizers for plants. If you add acid to paper it becomes see-through. It's often added to toilet paper. Fortunately the acid is washed off later otherwise it could be appallingly uncomfortable. But that's not the only thing sulphuric acid can do...

The acid test

An acid test is when you use a specially-treated paper called litmus to detect acid. The paper goes red if there's acid around. But in 1949 the acid test was one of lies versus truth and the issue was murder!

In 1949 businessman John Haigh was charged with murder. He had disposed of his victim's body in an appallingly horrible way by dumping it in sulphuric acid. Haigh had boasted to police that there would be nothing left. As he said at the time:

But Haigh was wrong. The acid had not destroyed the evidence. There were a few grisly tell-tale bits remaining – and a complete set of plastic false teeth. These were promptly identified by the dentist of the murdered woman.

Haigh then admitted getting rid of five more bodies using the same method. He went on trial at Lewes Assizes. The jury took eighteen minutes to reach their verdict and John Haigh was executed.

Appalling acid poisons

1 Rhubarb leaves contain poisonous oxalic (ox-al-ic) acid. It's there to poison caterpillars that fancy nibbling it. Luckily, there's less poison in the stalk and it's destroyed when it's stewed.

I'VE SUDDENLY LOST MY APPETITE

2 Bee stings contain acid and that's why they hurt. You can neutralize a bee sting with bicarbonate of soda because this is alkaline.

3 But put alkali on a wasp sting and it hurts more than ever. Wasp sting poison is alkaline not acid! And if you want to know more about alkalis you'll need some basic base facts.

Bases fact file

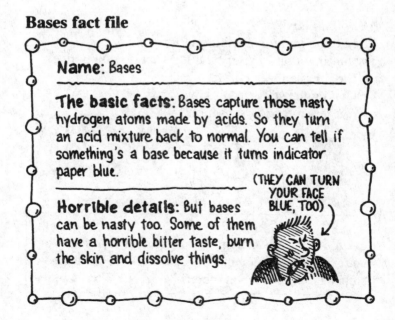

Name: Bases

The basic facts: Bases capture those nasty hydrogen atoms made by acids. So they turn an acid mixture back to normal. You can tell if something's a base because it turns indicator paper blue.

(THEY CAN TURN YOUR FACE BLUE, TOO)

Horrible details: But bases can be nasty too. Some of them have a horrible bitter taste, burn the skin and dissolve things.

Dare you discover ... the secret of sherbet?

You will need:

50 g (2 ounces) citric acid crystals (You can buy them from a chemist's shop.)

25 g (1 ounce) bicarbonate of soda

175 g (7 ounces) icing sugar

All you do is:

Mix all the ingredients thoroughly.

Try putting a bit in your mouth. What do you notice?

a) The tongue turns purple.

b) The tongue starts to dissolve.

c) You feel a fizzing sensation.

Answer: c) The acid lemon juice and the alkaline bicarbonate of soda react together to produce carbon dioxide gas. If you add sherbet to a drink you can make it taste fizzy.

282

Salty secrets

When you mix an acid and a base they react to make ... a salt. A salt isn't simply the stuff you put on your french fries. If you look closely at a salt you'll see an arrangement of tiny shapes. It's a collection of crucial crystals.

IT'S TRUE!

Crucial crystals

Here's a question to mystify your teacher: What have metals, gems, bones and computer chips got in common?

Answer: they all contain crystals. Some of them are crucially important.

A smashing discovery

In 1781 René-Just Haüy was having a rather chaotic time. He dropped a calcite stone on the floor. It shattered into identically shaped pieces. Intrigued he smashed the broken bits even more with a hammer. This produced smaller fragments that were still of the same intricate shape. He was looking at crystals!

Crystals fact file

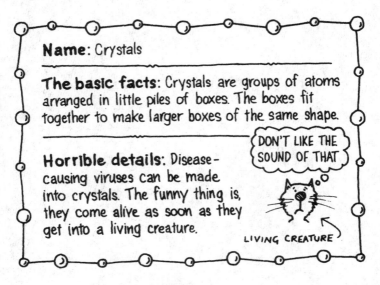

Name: Crystals

The basic facts: Crystals are groups of atoms arranged in little piles of boxes. The boxes fit together to make larger boxes of the same shape.

Horrible details: Disease-causing viruses can be made into crystals. The funny thing is, they come alive as soon as they get into a living creature.

DON'T LIKE THE SOUND OF THAT

LIVING CREATURE

A sick discovery

This discovery was made by Wendell M. Stanley (1904-1971). He infected some leaves with the tobacco mosaic virus. He mashed up the dried leaves and found that the virus had turned into nasty needle-like crystals.

> **Bet you never knew!**
> Salt is made up of crystals. If you look at salt through a microscope you'll see them as a pile of little boxes.

Salty secrets

1 Salt contains the elements sodium and chlorine. Both chemicals are poisonous but strangely a little salt is vital for your health!

2 In the Middle Ages people used to baptize their babies in salt water. It was thought to bring good luck.

3 In France an unpopular tax on salt helped to trigger the French Revolution and the execution of thousands of people.

4 Salt is a major problem in parts of Asia. As swampy land dries out salt is left in the soil and kills the plants.
5 But that's nothing to the Dead Sea. This inland lake is the saltiest place in the world. It's so salty no fish can live there!

Crucial crystals quiz

Crystals can be used for loads of crucial jobs but some of their uses you wouldn't believe. Which of these is too incredible to be true?

1 Diamonds were used to make spacecraft windows for a trip to Venus.

2 Diamonds are used to make lenses for protective goggles.

3 Rubies have been used to make lasers.

4 Crystals are used in some hospitals to kill germs.

5 Scientists are investigating using energy locked up in the atoms of crystals to power space craft.

6 Crystals were used in early radio sets.

Answers: 1 TRUE. The diamonds didn't heat up in the planet's fiery atmosphere. **2 FALSE 3 TRUE.** The atoms in the crystals take in energy and let it out in one intense beam of light. **4 and 5 FALSE 6 TRUE.** The crystals were used to control electrical currents inside the radio.

Bet you never knew!
The colours in gems are due to tiny amounts of other chemicals. For example, a bit of chromium turns a crystal pink. A bit more chromium makes a ruby red. Most diamonds don't contain other chemicals and that's why they're clear.

Crucial diamond facts

1 Diamonds are made from carbon atoms. 250 km (155 miles) below ground intense heat and pressure force the atoms into a cage-like shape.

2 Diamonds are so hard the only thing that cuts them is ...

another diamond. Their strength makes diamonds ideal for cutting all kinds of metals. You'll also find diamonds on the end of dentists' drills (that's if you dare look)!

3 The gems are sometimes spat out by volcanoes. This is why diamond mines are dug into volcanic rock.

4 It was Lavoisier who discovered that diamonds are made of carbon. He used a giant magnifying glass that focused the rays of a hot sun onto a diamond. Suddenly it disappeared in a puff of carbon-dioxide gas. The carbon in the gas came from the diamond.

5 Scientists believe that up to 15 per cent of the planets Uranus and Neptune could be made up of diamonds. If you could find a way to get your hands on them you could become the richest person in the Solar System.

6 Diamonds are so mysterious that it's not surprising that there are many diamond myths. But BEWARE – some diamonds are cursed with deadly misfortune. Here's the sinister story of just one famous gem.

A deadly diamond

It was a large blue diamond – unmatched in its beauty and rarity.

No one knew its origin. Some whispered that it was the eye of an Indian goddess – stolen from a temple. And perhaps it was cursed too.

It was sold to the French King and was worn by Queen Marie Antoinette. In 1793 she was executed and her priceless stone was stolen!

In 1830 the gem was sold in a London auction. It was bought by a banker – Henry Hope. But Hope died penniless with his business empire in ruins.

A young Prince bought the diamond for his girlfriend. He later shot her.

A Turkish Sultan bought the stone. A few weeks afterwards he was forced to give up his throne.

A wealthy Greek bought the diamond but he was killed when he drove his car off a cliff.

The next owner was an American millionairess who wore the diamond in a necklace. Her husband went mad and two of her children died in tragic accidents.

The next owner of the necklace wisely gave it to a museum. And that's when the story should have ended.

But in 1962 a museum curator took the diamond to Paris for an exhibition ... in his pocket! His plane landed four hours late and the man's car was involved in an accident. The curator wasn't hurt but he never took the stone anywhere again.

Mind you, diamonds can threaten disaster for other reasons too.

A cut above the rest

Premier Diamond Mine, South Africa, 26 January 1905
Frederick Wells couldn't believe his eyes. Embedded in the wall of the freshly dug pit was a prize worth dying for. A huge diamond weighing perhaps 500 grammes

(1lb, 2 oz) – that's as big as a man's fist. In a few moments the dazed mine boss was frantically digging out the diamond with his penknife.

It was the largest diamond ever found and it was fit for a king. So the government bought it for $750,000 to give to King Edward VII of Britain as a birthday present.

HAPPY BIRTHDAY DEAR YOUR MAJESTY, HAPPY BIRTHDAY TO YOU

Now came the tricky bit. The diamond was a rough stone. For its true beauty to shine, the stone had to be split in pieces and each piece carefully cut and polished.

So it was sent to Mr J. Asscher – the most famous diamond cutter in Amsterdam. For months Asscher studied the gem trying to guess how it would split. If he was right, the diamonds would be objects of priceless value. But if he was wrong the gem would shatter into fragments. The King would lose everything – but then so would Asscher. His business would be ruined because no one would ever trust him with their diamonds again. He would be a laughing stock and a famous failure.

With shaking hands Asscher set the gem against a wedge. He made a tiny notch in what he hoped was the right spot. He took a chisel and slowly and painstakingly placed it at the precise angle in the notch. His mouth was dry and there were tiny beads of sweat running down his forehead. His hand trembled violently as he picked up a mallet. This was the moment of truth...

Would the diamond shatter? Would it split to perfection? Asscher would never forget the next few moments...

He hit the chisel with all his strength.

The steel chisel shattered.

The diamond was too hard.

Asscher was led away to hospital. He was laughing like a madman and his nerves were shattered – even if the diamond wasn't.

Meanwhile, just thinking about the priceless gem made his skin crawl. But he was determined to try again.

After weeks of treatment Asscher felt well enough to return to work. At last the dreaded day dawned. This time a doctor was on hand to provide first aid.

Asscher closed his eyes and clenched his teeth. He gripped the chisel in one sweaty hand.

Then he struck...

The diamond split cleanly in just the right place. But Asscher was lying on the floor. He had fainted!

The Cullinan diamond was cut into 105 beautifully polished diamonds – each one worth millions of pounds. Two of these are in the English crown jewels. The finest and largest diamond is the Star of Africa which holds pride of place in the royal sceptre.

DIY diamonds

Not surprisingly, many chemists have tried to make their own diamonds. But chaos often ensued. For example, Scotsman J.B. Hannay blew up his laboratory in 1880 after heating carbon in an iron tube.

Henri Moissan, the discoverer of fluoride, knew that diamonds are sometimes found in meteorites. So he decided to make his own shooting star. He melted a lump of iron with carbon in the middle. But he didn't find any diamonds.

Eventually, scientists learnt how to make diamonds. You've got to heat graphite to 1,500°C (2732°F) under massive pressure. Thousands of tiny crystals appear. But it takes a week of this treatment to make even a small diamond.

Dare you discover ... how to make your own crystals?

You will need:
a beaker
salt and warm water
food colour

All you do is:
1 Mix the salt and water in the beaker so that the salt dissolves.
2 Add the food colour.
3 Leave the mixture in a warm, sunny place for about two days. Sit back and wait for a reaction.
So what happens?
a) You return to find priceless gems have formed in your beaker.

b) The mixture evaporates down and coloured crystals appear.
c) You can fish some shiny lumps out of the beaker with a spoon.

Bet you never knew!

Buckminsterfullerene is the name given to a form of carbon discovered in 1985. It forms hollow crystals in the shape of footballs. They're named after Richard Buckminster Fuller (1895-1983) an American architect who designed domes of this shape for factories and exhibition buildings. Buckminsterfullerene is a bit of a mouthful, so scientists call the shapes "bucky balls" for short. They sound very rare and exotic – but they're not. You'll find them in boring old soot.

Mind you – there's a lot of soot wafting about in the next chapter. It's made by combustion (that's the posh word for burning) and fiery explosions!

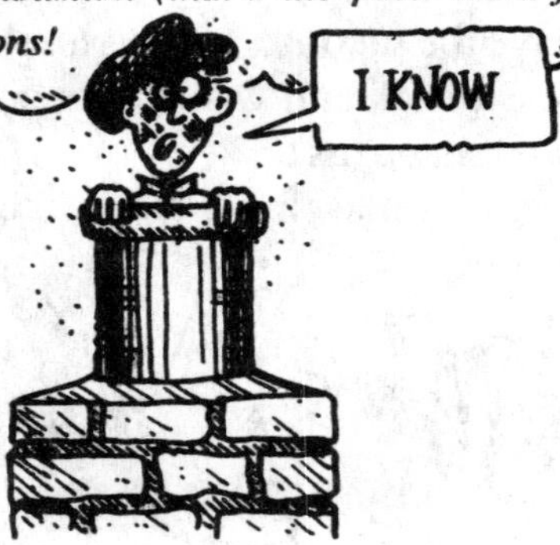

I KNOW

Bangs and burning

Burning and explosions are nothing out of the ordinary. They're just chemical reactions that get ... a bit out of hand. For centuries people have found bangs and burning useful. Read on for an explosive story.

A burning issue

Thousands of years ago one of your ancestors made the greatest discovery of all. Fire. Without it school dinners would be even worse – just raw veg and very tough meat. There'd be no heat and no electricity because this form of power depends on burning coal or oil. There'd be no metals because there would no metal smelting (apart from gold, that is!). And your school would be built of mud because without fire you can't make bricks and glass.

Burning fact file

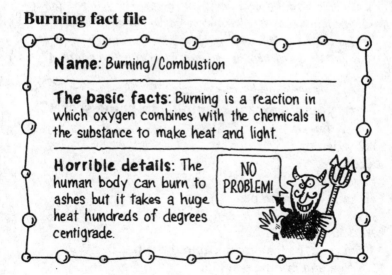

Name: Burning/Combustion

The basic facts: Burning is a reaction in which oxygen combines with the chemicals in the substance to make heat and light.

Horrible details: The human body can burn to ashes but it takes a huge heat hundreds of degrees centigrade.

NO PROBLEM!

Chaotic chemical expressions

Answer: His beard's on fire.

Bet you never knew!
1 Fire sucks in air to make light and heat.
2 A flame gives off heat and light energy. The yellow bit of a candle flame consists of unburned carbon from the candle.
3 Gas can burn with a clear flame if there's enough oxygen to burn all the gas. There are no messy bits of leftover carbon.

Dare you discover ... lemon's burning secret?

You will need:
half a lemon
a cup
paper
an empty fountain pen

All you do is:
1 Squeeze the lemon juice into the cup.
2 Wash and dry the pen nib.

3 Dip the pen in the lemon juice and write a few words on the paper.

4 Hold the paper in front of a warm radiator. The writing appears on the page. Why?

a) The heat makes the paper whiter so you can see the writing.

b) The heat makes the paper darker so that the writing shows up.

c) The heat makes the lemon juice darker so you can see it.

> **Answer: c)** Lemon juice burns at a lower temperature than paper. This fact is very useful for sending your own secret messages.

Fearsome phosphorous

One chemical that burns easily is phosphorous. For centuries doctors prescribed this poisonous chemical as a medicine. The doctors thought that it must be good for you because it glows in the dark! Then an inventor discovered phosphorous matches.

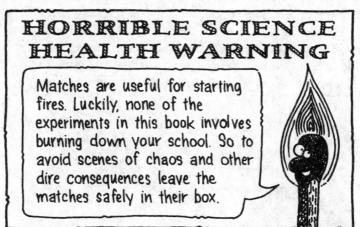

HORRIBLE SCIENCE HEALTH WARNING

Matches are useful for starting fires. Luckily, none of the experiments in this book involves burning down your school. So to avoid scenes of chaos and other dire consequences leave the matches safely in their box.

Strike a light

In 1826 John Walker, a chemist from Stockton-on-Tees, England was stirring potassium carbonate and antimony with a stick. When he scraped the stick on a stone floor to get rid of the chemical blob on its end, the stick caught fire. John Walker had met his match.

DRAT! THAT'S THE FOURTH COAT THIS WEEK!

John decided to sell his new inventions and strike it rich. At that time people carried tinder boxes containing flint and steel to make sparks and a bit of dried fungus to burn. Now everyone had money to burn on the new matches!

But the new matches were deadly. If the air got warm and moist, the matches burst into flames. They sometimes set fire to people's pockets and made poisonous fumes. A few customers got more than their fingers burnt.

STRIKE A LIGHT!

And there was an even more terrible price to pay. Phosphorous slowly poisoned the girls who made matches. Entering the body through rotten teeth it caused a ghastly bone disease nick-named "phossy jaw".

When these facts came to light social reformers campaigned to ban the matches. In 1888 the workers went on strike (that means not working, not striking matches, silly). But people didn't stop using the matches until they were banned in 1912.

Nowadays we use "safety matches". They were developed as early as the 1840s. Basically you've got two reactive chemicals – potassium chlorate on the match head and a phosphorous-based chemical on the striking surface. Since the chemicals don't mix until the match is struck they should be safe enough. But the early safety matches didn't quite get it right. They sometimes had the habit of exploding all by themselves.

Nowadays in Britain alone people use 100,000,000,000 (one hundred thousand million) matches every year! That's enough wood for 70,000 trees.

Mad machines – the self-igniting match

Here's a marvellous match-saving (and tree-saving) invention. A nineteenth-century French scientist made this bell-shaped box.

MATCH PULLS OUT FROM TOP OF BELL

AH OUI!

As you pull out the match, a spark sets fire to the chemical inside the box. Return the match to its hole and the flame goes out. Brilliant!

JUST WATCH WHERE YOU USE IT!

Explosions fact file

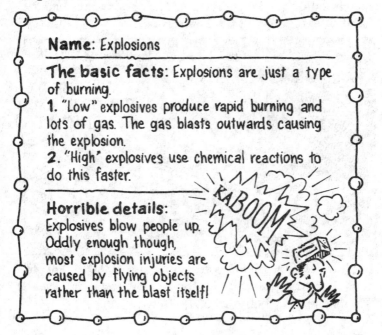

Name: Explosions

The basic facts: Explosions are just a type of burning.

1. "Low" explosives produce rapid burning and lots of gas. The gas blasts outwards causing the explosion.

2. "High" explosives use chemical reactions to do this faster.

Horrible details:
Explosives blow people up. Oddly enough though, most explosion injuries are caused by flying objects rather than the blast itself!

KABOOM

Chaotic chemists' hall of fame:

Sir Humphry Davy (1778-1829) Nationality: British
Sir Humphry on schooling...

I'm glad I wasn't worked too hard. It gave me more time to think for myself.

Now let that be a lesson to teachers everywhere. In fact, Davy taught himself science and he must have done a good job. Within five years of reading his first chemistry book he was a Professor of Chemistry at the Royal Institution!

In 1815 he went to Newcastle to investigate the problem of explosions in coal mines. After studying samples of the gas, he found that the explosions were caused by the intense heat of the flame. So he designed a lamp:

GAUZE TAKES IN HEAT AND STOPS THE GAS EXPLODING

STRONG GLASS PROTECTS FLAME FROM GAS

But as mines were getting safer, a soldier's life was getting more dangerous.

A potted history of gunpowder

1 A seventh-century Chinese alchemist described how to make gunpowder from sulphur, saltpetre and charcoal.

2 Saltpetre is found in rotting pig manure. Early gunpowder makers boiled the disgusting mess and then cooled it to make saltpetre crystals.

3 Licking the mixture checked the crystals for unwanted salt. Eurk!

4 For six centuries the Chinese guarded their secret. Then Europeans somehow managed to steal the recipe and invented cannon.

And muskets that could fire through armour...

And bombs to put under city walls...

5 Wars would never be the same again. The problem with gunpowder was that it filled battlefields with thick smoke. So you couldn't see anything...

6 Nowadays gunpowder is found in fireworks and a similar chemical is used to preserve tinned meat.

IT'S LOVELY GEORGE, WHAT IS IT?

A FIREWORK OF COURSE

Bet you never knew!
One type of explosive was invented after another bit of chemical chaos. Christian Schönbein (1799-1868) was experimenting in his kitchen when he spilt a mixture of nitric and sulphuric acid. So he snatched his wife's apron to mop it up. Keen to avoid an explosive situation with his wife the chaotic chemist left the apron to dry. It dried ... and exploded! Schönbein had discovered nitro-cellulose – the world's first exploding fabric.

Bangs and blasts!

1 The bang in your Christmas cracker is caused by mercuric fulminate. In 1800, its inventor was injured during a lecture as he tried to show it off. Luckily, you only get a tiny bit in a cracker or your party would go with a very loud bang!

2 Another explosive is TNT – otherwise known as trinitrotoluene (try-nite-tro-toll-you-lene). One TNT molecule will produce a blast one thousand times its size. It just takes a little shock to set it off. Mind you – a blast like that will give you more than a little shock.

306

3 Amazingly, one kilogram of butter stores as much energy in the bonds between its atoms as the same quantity of TNT! But butter tastes nicer on toast and it doesn't blow up either.

The man who made a bomb

Dynamite was discovered by Swedish inventor Alfred Nobel. The blasting power comes from nitroglycerine which is an oily mix of glycerine and acids used by Schönbein. Although he became one of the world's richest men, Alfred Nobel wasn't a bundle of laughs. He was tormented by a guilty conscience. Here's what his diary might have looked like.

∽1865∾

Dear Diary

It's _all_ got out of hand. Explosives are fantastic and fascinating and fun, and I've never been afraid of them ... but today I've discovered just how dangerous, dreadful ... and deadly they can be. There was this explosion in the factory.

All my work's destroyed. And, most terrible of all, my brother is dead. That's what explosives really do. They kill people. It's horrible. And now I'll never see my brother or speak to him again.

I'll never touch explosives again, either! If only Dad hadn't got me started, what with his underwater mines, I'd never have thought about playing around with that nasty nitroglycerine stuff.

No, that's it, finished. No more loud bangs for me, not even so much as a pop. I'm going to forget all about the amazing effects of playing with chemicals, loud bangs, fireworks, sparks flying . . . It's just too dangerous. But it's so fascinating, too, maybe I could just play around a little, from time to time. I could try and do something good with explosives. Maybe I could invent one that didn't do anyone any harm. I could invent a safe explosive. Yes, that's it, that's what I'll do!

∽1866∾

I'm brilliant! I've cracked it. I've invented a safe explosive that will definitely make the world a better place. They'll use it in mines and, well, anywhere, really. And the brilliant thing about it is that it won't blow up if you accidentally drop it. It's so simple to make. I just mixed that nasty nitroglycerine with kieselguhr (made from the ground-up skeletons of tiny sea creatures). That was all! The kieselguhr absorbs the chemicals in the nitroglycerine. Then you fire an explosive cap to set it all off. I'm going to call my new invention - "dynamite".

_me_

<u>Disaster!</u> My wonderful life-saving invention has gone horribly wrong. It's out of control. It's made me rich beyond my wildest dreams, but what good is the money when they use my invention for weapons of war? I wish I'd never discovered it. I want to be remembered for good deeds, not bad.

But if I can't get it right, maybe someone else can. I'm going to use my fortune to fund a really special prize. It will be presented every year, and given to people whose inventions do truly great things for science, the arts . . . and peace. That should make the world a better place . . . shouldn't it?

But can chemicals really make the world a better place?

Chemical chaos?

Chemicals cause chaos – if we don't look after them properly, if they explode at the wrong moment, or if we let them loose without knowing what they'll do to the environment. So are we cooking up a chaotic chemical catastrophe? Or is it just the chaos of invention?

As ever, it's always the bad news that hits the headlines first. (You don't hear so much about the exciting new discoveries that happen all the time.)

A DEADLY DISASTER!

11 December 1979 Just before midnight, 106 train wagons of dangerous chemicals jumped the rails in Mississauga, Ontario, Canada.

One wagon contained 90 tonnes (89 tons) of chlorine, 11 others were full of easy-to-burn propane gas. Witnesses report scenes of chaos with massive fires raging out of control. One carriage exploded at once and another was blasted 750 metres (820 yards) away.

A quarter of a million people were forced to flee their homes as the chlorine wagon began leaking deadly fumes. Firefighters on the scene are working round the clock in a desperate bid to plug the leak. Their first attempts have failed to make the area safe. Meanwhile the evacuees wait anxiously for news of when they can return to their homes...

Luckily, the first explosion had thrown the chlorine high into the air and away from nearby cities. The locals were not in any danger, but it was days before the experts could confirm the air was safe. Others haven't been so lucky. Although the chemical industry has strict safety standards, horrible accidents can happen. In Bhopal, India, in 1984 two thousand people were killed by a poison gas cloud following an explosion at a chemical factory. And there's more bad news...

A sticky situation

Imagine crude oil – it began as the rotten bodies of plants and animals squashed under the ground millions of years ago. It's thick, black, sticky and very messy and people risk their lives to get at it. They drill holes in the beds of stormy oceans and venture into barren deserts.

And why? Because oil is horribly useful. You can make it into substances such as petrol to power cars, bitumen to surface roads and the raw ingredients of plastics.

Trouble is – like many chemicals, oil causes chaos when it gets out of human control. Oil spills wipe out wildlife and turn golden sandy beaches into black, slimy wastelands. And car exhausts cause problems too.

How's this for progress...?

The 1900s...

Smog made from coal smoke and fog caused pollution in cities. In Britain smoky coal fires were banned in the 1950s.

The 1990s...

Smog made from car exhaust fumes caused pollution in cities. What do you think should be done about it?

The good news

Although chemistry seems horribly chaotic at times, chemistry is also incredibly creative. The creative ideas of chemists can make most people's wildest dreams look rather tame. Just imagine a spacecraft made from a material that resists temperatures of 10,000°C (18,032°F) without melting.

If your reaction is to say, "What will those science fiction writers think of next?" you'll be amazed to know that this substance already exists. It was invented in 1993. And here are a few more substances that seem too good to be true.

Fantastic facts

Chemists have invented...

1 A superacid called fluoro-antimonic (flewer-ro-anti-mon-ic) acid with twenty thousand trillion (20,000,000,000,000,000,000,000) times the dissolving power of the most powerful concentrated sulphuric acid. Keep your fingers clear of that!

2 A sponge called H-spon invented in 1974. It's so good at mopping up spills that it can hold up to 1,300 times its own weight in moisture.

I'M IMPRESSED

3 A new type of sugarlump 650 times sweeter than ordinary sugar. It's called talin and made from seeds of the West African Katemfe plant.

TOO MUCH SUGAR, DEAR?

4 Crystals called zeolites in the shape of tiny sieves that separate individual atoms in a chemical. They're a compound of aluminium, silicon, water and metals.

And there's more good news...
Chemists can actually use their chemical knowledge to tackle the chaos of chemical pollution.
1 Many of the world's cars contain catalytic (cat-a-lit-ic) converters. The metal honeycomb shape is coated with platinum. This traps the nasty chemicals produced by the car's engine and breaks them down into harmless chemicals such as water.
2 Ordinary petrol contains lead – added to stop the car engine making knocking sounds. Unfortunately lead in car exhaust fumes is enough to take your breath away. Don't forget lead is poisonous! So chemists have developed lead-free petrol and you can use it in your catalytic converter.
3 Every year people chuck thousands of tonnes of plastics in deep holes in the ground. What a waste. But in 1993 a factory opened in Britain that turns plastic back into the oils that they were made of originally. So now you can make old plastic into new plastic.

4 You remember that hole in the ozone layer caused by chlorine-based gases? They were used to put the squirting power into aerosol cans. But they've been banned and chemists have developed safer gases to use instead. So now you can spray on deodorant without causing a stink for the environment.

THANK GOODNESS FOR THAT!

The chaotic truth

It's not chemicals that cause chaos – it's *humans*. We make chemicals. We store them, we use them – ultimately we are responsible for what they do.

We can use them for good or allow them to cause chaos and destruction. The decision is ours. Here's what one chemist had to say on the subject. Pierre Curie (1859-1906) and his wife Marie (1867-1934) discovered the element radium. Pierre said:

We might still consider that in criminal hands radium might become very dangerous . . . (but) I am among those who believe that humanity will derive more good than evil from new discoveries.

We hardly know what lies in the future. Except that out of the chaos of chemistry will emerge even more amazing and incredible inventions. And the future will be more fantastic and hopefully brighter than ever before. And that's the chaotic truth!